CONCEALED CARRY
FOR WOMEN

GILA HAYES

Published by

Gun Digest® Books, an imprint of F+W Media, Inc.
Krause Publications • 700 East State Street • Iola, WI 54990-0001
715-445-2214 • 888-457-2873
www.krausebooks.com

To order books or other products call toll-free 1-800-258-0929
or visit us online at www.gundigeststore.com

ISBN-13: 978-1-4402-3600-6
ISBN-10: 1-4402-3600-3

Cover Design by Al West
Designed by Sandi Carpenter
Edited by Corrina Peterson

Printed in the United States of America

CONTENTS

FOREWORD

You've probably never thought much about protecting yourself until now. You feel vulnerable, alone, threatened. You know an attack will be over before the police arrive.

The uncomfortable, unavoidable, and simple fact is that women face more threats to their safety than do men. Rape, stalking and abduction are rarely visited upon the male of our species.

Millions of women have made the decision to be responsible for their own security. They are buying guns and getting their carry permits, but, just as with their male counterparts, they rarely receive the training needed to be competent. Training is the key to learn the basics of firearms operation as well as self-defense techniques, but there are some challenges–actually quite a few, as it turns out–unique to women who carry guns.

Over the 18 years I've hosted *Tom Gresham's Gun Talk* radio show, I've taken calls from women all over the country, asking questions about whether it's smart to get a gun, what kind of gun to get, how to carry and the issues particular to women who carry. In *Concealed Carry for Women*, Gila Hayes covers the basics of handgun and equipment choices and techniques of shooting. She also addresses issues unique to women. Should I? Why? Can I? How do I? What if? What will people think? How can I carry a defensive handgun and still dress like a woman?

Women have been mastering complex challenges for eons. Effectively and safely carrying a gun is no more difficult than the load each of them now carries in everyday living.

Gila Hayes has been teaching women to protect themselves for decades. She is an accomplished writer who has perfected making complex subjects easy to understand. It's my pleasure to call her a friend. I've spent time on the shooting range with her and her husband, Marty, at their training facility in Washington State. Simply put, she knows what she's talking about. She's a shooter, a trainer, a constant student who learns from other trainers and from her own students.

Concealed Carry for Women is an easy read of a serious subject. With nearly every turn of the page there is an "I never thought of that" nugget. This is a work you will reread several times, getting more with each visit.

That you are reading this indicates you have made the decision to protect yourself or that someone who loves you has given you this book because he or she wants you to stay safe.

Gila would be the first to tell you this book, as good as it is, just gets you started. It's the first step on a journey that will change your life. Self reliant. Confident. Safer. More aware. You will be different.

Congratulations on crossing over from being dependent to becoming self reliant. I can think of no better way to begin the transformation than with this excellent book.

Tom Gresham
Host, "Tom Gresham's Gun Talk" radio show

ACNOWLEDGEMENTS

Tom Gresham graciously wrote the foreword for this book, despite the request to do so coming during a demanding period in this busy man's life. How generous, and how typically "Tom." Tom's influence on me started a long time before his assistance on this effort, through his *Gun Talk* radio program, on which he graciously let me appear several times, and later granting me several very fun guest appearances on his TV show *Personal Defense TV*. In addition, I have had the privilege of turning the tables and interviewing Tom for several articles in my own monthly online journal at www.armedcitizensnetwork.org/our-journal.

Tom has long exerted a strong, positive influence on me and my opinions and how I conduct myself as an armed citizen and a firearms trainer. One of the lessons he taught me simply through example came up during an episode of *Personal Defense TV* that I filmed with him. Before we started, Tom explained that, as the host, he would assume the role of the learner to whom I was to address my observations. Sometimes he acted as if he knew far less than he actually knows, and sometimes he portrayed common mistakes made by beginners. He explained that he had no ego to protect, stressing that his foremost goal for the program was teaching armed citizens how to be better and safer shooters. Clearly Tom would do what was necessary to create many teachable moments.

I have often reflected on Tom's willingness to play that role without concern that viewers would mock or disparage him. I have borrowed Tom's wonderful attitude throughout this book whenever "Don't Ever Do This!" illustrations needed to be made, knowing that many readers will learn more thoroughly from pictures than from wordy admonitions. So let me say thank you, Tom, for showing me how to be a better communicator, not only in this aspect but in many others, as well. You are my inspiration!

Compared to all of the other gun and holster books for sale, this one is somewhat atypical. Women love to learn by example, so instead of putting too much focus on hardware and accessories, I've approached sharing information along the lines of "this is a common holster type and here is how it is used best by women." The vagaries of commerce in uncertain economic times convince me that it is more sensible to show concealed carry methods that have worked well for women, from which the astute reader can shop for similar products or simply take the picture and description to a holster maker and ask that the leatherworker make a holster with the desirable attributes.

Naturally, in this kind of communication, you can't beat a picture. If the old adage that a picture is worth a thousand words is true, I owe my photographers, Bob Jackson and Grant Cunningham, far more than they will ever receive in financial remuneration for the hundreds of photographs they created to illustrate holsters, firearms use and firearms features in use by women.

As our readers already know, women come in all shapes and sizes, so guns and gear that work splendidly for one woman may or may not work so well for another. The women who help illustrate this book, Melissa DeYoung, Kathy Jackson and Diane Walls are a lot more than pretty faces. They are firearms instructors and women who carry guns every day. Their contributions to this book are beyond value, and words are not enough to express my gratitude for their generous advice and assistance. Also much more than handsome faces are the male firearms instructors Tom Walls and Frank DeYoung, who appear briefly where an illustration or comparison required the masculine touch.

On the topic of gentlemen, my husband and business partner Marty Hayes is influential not only in the firearms and shooting skills discussed in this book, but also as a force of encouragement and patience through the writing process. Likewise, my editor at Gun Digest Books, Corrina Peterson, never failed to come through quickly with answers and information, and without her vision, I would have never undertaken this project.

Many trainers have been influential in my growth as a shooter and instructor. These include Marty Hayes, Massad Ayoob, John and Vicki Farnam, Clint Smith, Ken Hackathorn, Chuck Taylor and Tom Givens to name only a few. I could not help but think of Tom Givens during the photography sessions, in which we tried repeatedly to illustrate failures of carry methods for the camera, and often did not succeed in failing even when setting up holster and clothing combinations we would never wear out in public. Tom's words echoed in my mind, as I remembered him telling me that only the armed citizen is aware of his or her self-defense guns, and that the public is largely oblivious to our bumps and bulges. Tom, you were right!

The influential people who have guided my development in the firearms industry for the past 25 years comprise a list too long to publish, and besides, it is time to move on to the information for which you bought this book.

In closing, thank you readers, for your interest in firearms and self defense for women. By creating a class of resourceful, prepared and skillful women, we are changing both the reality and the perception of women as weak and easy victims. Though this effort is not yet complete, we continue by example to influence other women who are ready to take charge of their own safety. There is no stronger teacher.

Let us never give up.
Gila Hayes
February 2013
Onalaska, WA

YOU ARE
NOT ALONE!

Do you own a gun? Are you thinking that getting a gun may be the sensible response to the danger of violence against you and your family? If so, you're among thousands of other American women who recognize that when danger is immediate, only the individual threatened can take the actions necessary to protect self and family, since in the time required for help to arrive, the crime can usually be completed and the assailant departed. Numerous self-defense tools and techniques are available and I'm proud to say that these days, many women practice a variety of defense techniques spanning awareness, avoidance, deterrence and fighting back with defenses ranging from physical, chemical and, when left with no other option, using firearms to prevent being sexually assaulted, maimed or killed.

Make no mistake, American women own and shoot firearms. Polling by the well-respected Gallup organization showed in an October 2011 study that 43 percent of women surveyed answered affirmatively when asked if there are guns in their households, and 23 percent of women polled said they personally own firearms. Anecdotal reports from gun retailers show that women are buying guns in ever-increasing numbers, as well.[1]

Self defense heads the list of reasons women give for obtaining guns and learning to shoot. While beginning shooters often focus their skill acquisition initially on home defense, it is not long before the realization dawns that while buffering oneself against violent crime at home is important, the exposure to and variety of dangers encountered when we are out in public are even harder to predict and counter. Carrying a concealed handgun to keep a means of defense immediately available is a common and effective self-defense provision many Americans practice. Handgun manufacturers, recognizing how many people carry self-defense handguns, have vastly expanded the options in guns that are small and light enough to carry on your person all your waking hours. Indeed, the ubiquity of small handguns suited to concealed, holstered carry underscores how many gun owners take a handgun along when they leave the relative safety of their homes. Such a large product line up could only survive if supported by a vital and enthusiastic consumer base.

As we will detail in a later chapter, advocates of armed self defense have worked hard to increase the number of states licensing concealed carry of handguns. At the time of this writing, only the State of Illinois and the District of Columbia lack legislation providing licensure for citizens carrying guns for self defense, and pro-gun activists are gaining ground in Illinois. Sadly, not all states with laws licensing concealed carry actually let citizens from all walks of life carry guns for self defense, whether through prohibitively expensive license fees, difficult to obtain training, or strict limits on where licensed carry is allowed. Too many Americans are thus rendered defenseless, and predators seem to know where easy victims can be found. Still, more Americans than not can legally practice some degree of concealed carry for their own protection. This is a far cry from 50 years ago!

How many concealed carry licensees are women? The data is incomplete, but we can make some pretty accurate guesses from the numbers available. In Kansas, for example, where licensing data sorted by gender was made available for the period of July 1, 2006, to Oct. 1, 2011,[2] just over 17 percent of all licenses were issued to women. In Arizona, reports show that over one quarter of licenses are issued to female applicants.[3]

WHY WOULD YOU WANT TO CARRY A GUN?

Why do women comprise such a strong percentage of the estimated eight million[4] citizens who are licensed to carry handguns? The answer is simple. Women frequently lack the size and strength to physically fight off a male assailant without being at something of a disadvantage, if not substantially out-classed by a stronger, larger man. While much can be said promoting hand-to-hand defensive tactics that deter or slow an assailant who is surprised to find a victim who is fighting back, against a very determined or mentally deranged predator, the risk of not prevailing in a physical fight is a serious and terrifying possibility. A gun immediately at hand balances the scales for the woman targeted for rape, abduction, murder or other violence. Access to the power of a firearm as part of a woman's personal defense strategy is just as important out in public as it is inside the home, and so we practice concealed carry.

Some armed citizens practice what is called open carry, which is, as the name implies, openly carrying a defensive handgun in a holster without covering it up with clothing or concealing it inside a pack or holster handbag. Many, but not all, states recognize the right of the citizen to openly carry firearms for personal protection, so open carry is not practiced nationwide. There is a time and a place for a variety of behaviors, and while much can be said in favor of exposing the American public to positive firearms ownership and use, open carry is not without uniquely inherent hazards. For women in particular, sacrificing the element of surprise when introducing a firearm into a confrontation turned violent carries a high price. Losing the element of surprise could change the outcome of the intended victim's self-defense efforts, especially if targeted for a disarming attempt first.

Furthermore, many women tend toward extreme privacy regarding their self-defense choices, not wishing to engage in endless arguments about whether there is ever a time or place in which shooting another human being is morally acceptable, or whether there exist such dangers as to merit carrying a gun. In my opinion, not advertising that you are carrying a handgun is wise. The armed woman has struggled with and answered questions about the justifiability of using deadly force in self defense, and she is under no obligation to defend her security choices to a society that too often does not place a high priority on her safety. A personal

> *The armed woman is under no obligation to defend her security choices to a society that too often does not place a high priority on her safety.*

defensive weapon carried concealed and out of sight accommodates preparation to fend off violent attack without facing challenges to defend such individual choices to strangers and others who have no right to question it but nonetheless will. A concealed handgun carried discreetly does not attract unwanted attention and remains unnoticed the vast majority of the time.

Carrying a defense gun wherever legal 24-7 requires a certain amount of ingenuity and an ongoing commitment to personal safety, since women's fashions tend toward tight, skimpy and revealing. If anyone told you that daily concealed carry would be easy, they probably haven't carried a self defense gun regularly for long. Conversely, if anyone told you it was impossible, those pessimists lacked the imaginative problem solving so ably demonstrated for decades by American women who carry guns.

What are some of the impediments that interfere with women carrying guns and protecting themselves? One of the most common problems women express about carrying a gun is lack of confidence and anxiety that they may harm themselves or another. Another concern is worry about failing to understand the law and subsequently doing something illegal, or simply behaving in opposition to the many messages broadcast by American society and government that prefer a dependent citizenry over self-sufficient individuals. Other women agonize about entering what they've always believed is a masculine enclave – marksmanship classes, shooting ranges and gun stores. It may even seem that most holsters and handguns are designed with men in mind, and these implements and accouterments seem wildly at odds with dresses, high heels and lacy clothing! Finally, women lead extremely demanding lives that pass through a number of phases, stretching from early adulthood into the child-raising phase, career-building, retirement and sometimes even raising second and third generations of their families, and then taking responsibility for the earlier generation of family members when they can no longer care for themselves. Leisure and recreation pursuits of a nearly endless variety take women into many environments requiring a nearly endless variety of dress codes. How, in Heaven's name, can a woman fit a handgun carried for personal protection into all of these situations?

It is easy to understand why some women simply find it easier to deny that they may someday have serious need for a firearm than to figure out how to integrate a gun into all those situations. Of course, women solve enormous and complex problems every day. In the pages to follow, we'll do the same with the foregoing issues and many more, and we'll do it in the same way women tackle the impossible every day – one step at a time.

So if you're interested in carrying a gun for self defense, would like to carry your gun more consistently, or have a home defense gun you wish you could begin to carry for personal protection in public, I think you will enjoy the following chapters as we explore these and many other issues. Are you ready for some creative problem-solving? Let's get started!

---

(1) While no gender specific gun sales statistics are available, 60 percent of firearm retailers responding to a National Shooting Sports Foundation survey reported an increase in female customers in 2011. Nearly one in four American women say they personally own a firearm, according to an October 2011 Gallup poll (http://www.gallup.com/poll/150353/Self-Reported-Gun-Ownership-Highest-1993.aspx). That survey indicated the highest gun ownership since the 1990s, with 43 percent of women reporting at least one firearm in their home and 23 percent saying the gun they reported is their own. (Half of American men own a firearm, the poll showed.)

(2) State of Kansas website http://ag.ks.gov/docs/documents/concealed-carry-applications-received-by-age-and-gender.pdf?sfvrsn=4

(3) State of Arizona website http://www.azdps.gov/Services/Concealed_Weapons/Statistics/

(4) Government Accountability Office, Report of July 2012, "Gun Control: States' Laws and Requirements for Concealed Carry Permits Vary across the Nation," at http://www.gao.gov/assets/600/592552.pdf

THE DECISION

Are you concerned about personal safety and self defense? What is most important to you? What will you fight to preserve? What self-defense methods are right for you? What issues do you need to work out if you are going to carry a gun for self defense?

"What could go wrong? I don't understand what you're so worried about!" Has anyone ever said that to you when you wondered if you would be safe going somewhere or participating in an event or activity? Denying dangers and risks is a common dodge people employ when the dangers appear to be just too big to tackle, and so it seems easier to deny them altogether. Before we make a brief survey of crime statistics, let me emphasize that identifying common crime trends is an important strategy in avoiding victimization. Knowing what to expect lets you interrupt an attack before the balance of power shifts entirely to the predator. Knowing what could happen makes it more likely that you will provide yourself with viable ways to defend against a determined assailant. Denial kills because those unwilling to admit to problems can never find and implement solutions.

What risks to personal safety should we worry about? How prevalent are assaults that cause women serious injury? When a struggle ensues, how likely is it that a female participant may be injured?

According to one survey, 39.0 percent of female physical assault victims, compared with 24.8 percent of male physical assault victims, reported being injured during their most recent physical assault.[1] The same researchers also indicate that stalking crimes are "more prevalent than previously thought" noting that approximately one million women are stalked annually in the United States. Stalking could be called a form of terrorism, because in itself, even if the offender never lays a hand on the victim, it robs the victim of peace of mind and the ability to get out and enjoy life. For more about this disturbing crime, see Dr. Lyn Bates book *Safety for Stalking Victims*.[2]

Though by no means the only kind of violence that women face, sexual assault is the one over which most women express the greatest worry. The National

Violence Against Women Survey (NVAWS) found that 17.6 percent of surveyed women were raped at some point in their lifetime. This particular study used a stringent definition of rape "that includes attempted and completed vaginal, oral and anal penetration achieved through the use or threat of force," so did not attempt to quantify attempted sexual assaults that were not included in that definition. The numbers increase if survey respondents are asked if they were ever forced into a sexual act.[3] Additional physical damage beyond the sexual injury is likely during sexual assault: 31.5 percent of female rape victims reported suffering other injuries, as well.

The emotional damage and mental health issues faced by sexual assault survivors are less easily quantified but must not be ignored. Many compelling books and articles, too many to list, make it clear that rape survivors often find maintaining relationships and employment difficult if not impossible in the aftermath of rape.

PREVENTIVE MEASURES

How can carrying a gun help you prevent these horrific crimes and or mitigate injury if the attack is unavoidable? The common sense conclusion that fighting back reduces incidences of injury has the support of scientific research in Gary Kleck and Jongyeon Tark's study *The Impact of Victim Self Protection on Rape Completion and Injury*, which finally put to rest the idiotic yet widely repeated assertion that resisting rape further endangered the intended victim. The study declared, "The injury rate figures show that while many crime victims are injured, resisting victims are less frequently and less seriously injured after taking some kind of protective action than non-resisting victims. In 556 rape/attempted rape incidents where victims resisted in some way, 54 percent of the rape attempts were completed, but only 19 percent of rape attempts with resisting victims were completed after the victim took self-protective (SP) actions, 26 percent involved the victim suffering some other (nonsexual) injury after taking SP actions, and 5 percent involved the victim suffering a serious (more serious than cuts and bruises) nonsexual injury. In contrast, among the 177 incidents involving victims who did not resist, 88 percent of incidents resulted in rape completion, 25 percent of such incidents resulted in a nonsexual injury, and 2.8 percent resulted in serious nonsexual injury."[4]

There is an especially disturbing side to violence against women we should acknowledge. Studying rape statistics shows how many of the assaults were perpetrated by persons known to the victim, and in particular enacted by intimate partners. Approximately 1.3 million women and 835,000 men are physically assaulted by an intimate partner annually in the United States (Tjaden & Thoennes, 2000, 2006). 22.1 percent of surveyed women, compared with 7.4 percent of surveyed men, reported that a current or former spouse, cohabiting partner, boyfriend, girlfriend or date had physically assaulted them in their lifetime.

Intimate partner homicides make up 40-50 percent of all murders of women in the United States according to city- and state-specific databases. In 70-80 percent of intimate partner homicides, no matter which partner was killed, the man physically abused the woman before the murder (Campbell et al., 2003).[5]

Issues about rape and physical abuse by an intimate partner may seem far removed from the question of carrying a gun for self defense. Women turn to guns for self defense for all kinds of reasons, including the danger of violence by an intimate partner, sometimes one from whom they have separated who has threatened their safety. For a woman who is rebuilding her personal world, learning how to defend against an abuser is an important step in regaining power over her own life. The psychology of a woman who assigns high enough priority to her own safety to pursue self-defense training, obtain various means of defense including firearms and holsters, and go to all the effort (yes, it is an effort) to always carry a gun reveals a considerable commitment to self preservation. In recovering from the depredations of an abusive relationship, that level of self-care is a good sign of growing self-esteem.

The other side of the rape statistics that show that women frequently are acquainted with their assailants puts the spotlight on the uncomfortable truth that professional acquaintances from work, people met at church, family members and relatives, and contacts from a variety of other activities can and do assault women who trust them. Does that mean we need to distrust everyone with whom we associate? Not at all! All it means is that as women, it is smart to maintain control over situations in which we are involved. Maintaining the power to control what is done to you includes consistently keeping available a means of self defense for circumstances that can arise if you've misjudged associates or acquaintances.

This is where firearms carried discreetly concealed have real benefit to you and other women. This is why licensed concealed carry is so vitally important to women who are taking and maintaining their place in the world. Some professions, especially stepping-stone jobs that make up the preliminary steps to the leadership positions we wish were more equally distributed to women, require travel. Instead of deciding to gamble with personal safety, a woman who carries a well-concealed handgun is able to go about the tasks she is given, perform them with her full concentration, and if those circumstances put her in danger's way, she has at hand the tools of individual defense. When you carry with you a means of preventing rape, abuse, assault and other life-threatening or maiming violence, you are better able to go places and do the things that promote your livelihood and you can live a more interesting and satisfying life.

I have read papers by social scientists suggesting that the fear of crime is more prevalent than actual incidences of crime.[6] The argument reminds me of the axiom that figures lie and liars figure. Personally, I am very guarded about making decisions about personal safety based on mere statistics, whether or not the numbers or studies support or oppose my beliefs. In making self-defense preparations, I would, instead, stay tuned in to local and regional crime news and pay close attention to injuries reported in the daily news and in year-end law enforcement arrest tabulations. Home invasions, assaults committed during property crimes like car jacking, and yes, sexual assaults still figure prominently in annual crime reports. I doubt social engineers will be quick to associate advances in concealed carry legislation with dropping crime statistics, but I believe, as John Lott asserts in his book *More Guns, Less Crime*,[7] that criminals prefer unarmed victims, and when it is unclear who is unarmed and who is armed, the entire population enjoys the benefit of the doubt when predators judge the risks too great. And while I'm relieved to see a decrease in crime,[8] I believe women continue to be targeted as easy victims because of the general perception that women won't engage in a physical fight. If we lack the means to combat assaults, the criminal's perception of women as easy prey may well be all too true.

WHAT WILL YOU FIGHT FOR?

Decisions about guns for self defense need to be based not only on a clear understanding of the dangers women face, but also on a reasonable expectation of the advantages that a firearm can give you if you are attacked. The decision to go armed needs also to take into consideration what you are willing to fight to the death to defend. In a society plagued by passivity and abdication of personal responsibility, women have been taught that it would be better to sacrifice themselves before harming another living creature—even if that creature is determined to kill or cripple them and other innocent lives. Such twisted thinking creates a terribly large pool of victims that it is safe to abuse.

Decisions about using deadly force to stop someone bent on killing or crippling you require considerable soul searching, yet must be resolved in advance if a gun is to be of much use in a self-defense emergency. You must ask yourself, "What am I willing to defend?" If you have children or other loved ones who are vulnerable, it is easy to imagine fighting tooth and nail to prevent harm to them. In reality, you are just as important and deserve a defense just as vigorous.

Take a few minutes to think about the people you treasure most. In all likelihood, the role you play in their lives is just as significant to them as they are to you! If you let a predator take your life or inflict such harm that you are not able to do all the things you do for those you love, losing you may hurt them as badly, if not worse, than if the predator had harmed them.

As a woman you have a lot of responsibilities. One responsibility is making smart decisions so that you remain alive and physically and mentally healthy for all those whose lives revolve around yours.

(1) Tjaden & Thoennes, 2000, https://www.ncjrs.gov/pdffiles1/nij/183781.pdf

(2) Bates, Lyn, Safety for Stalking Victims, http://www.aware.org/stalking/stalkbook.shtml

(3) Tjaden and Thoennes, 2006, https://www.ncjrs.gov/pdffiles1/nij/210346.pdf.

(4) Kleck and Tark, www.ncjrs.gov/pdffiles1/nij/grants/211201.pdf

(5) Campbell, https://www.ncjrs.gov/pdffiles1/jr000250e.pdf

(6) Stroud dissertation, epositories.lib.utexas.edu/bitstream/handle/2152/ETD-UT-2012-05-5425/STROUD-DISSERTATION.pdf?sequence=1.

(7) John Lott, More Guns; Less Crime, ISBN: 9780226493664, May 2010, University of Chicago Press: 1427 E. 60th Street Chicago, IL 60637, 773-702-7700 http://www.press.uchicago.edu/ucp/books/book/chicago/M/bo6686900.html

(8) http://www.time.com/time/magazine/article/0,9171,1963761,00.html

CONCEALED CARRY – THE LAW

Let's review the increasingly common laws allowing concealed carry and how important that legislation is to women who are serious about their self-defense provisions. Another facet of this discussion is the training many of the state concealed carry licensing laws require. Training is a great opportunity for women to learn about professional instructors, training facilities and firearms-related businesses that can play an important role in developing and becoming comfortable and competent in their self-defense skills.

Western movies make it sound like everyone in the United States carried a gun during pioneer times. While certain folks surely did go about their business armed, most often guns were carried openly. Sometimes, only open carry could be legally practiced. For example, in 1872, Wisconsin passed a law prohibiting concealed weapons carried by anyone but a law enforcement officer. It was not until 2011 that Wisconsin residents finally regained concealed carry rights. Gun rights historian Clayton Cramer cites legislation prohibiting concealed carry dating back to the 1800s. He explains that racism in the post-Civil War South contributed to gun restrictions that continued long into the 20th century.[1] Even in the "wild west," as early as the 1920s, California restricted concealed carry as one element in a larger gun restriction bill.[2] Today, many Californians are still denied the license required to legally carry a concealed handgun, because they live in a jurisdiction in which the chief law enforcement officer (a police chief or sheriff) opposes concealed carry.

Just two decades ago, only six states had laws that required authorities to issue a concealed carry license to any applicant meeting the state licensing requirements. These are known as "shall-issue" laws. At one time, most states' licensing terms were discretionary, meaning that the local chief law enforcement officer held the power to summarily grant or deny applications for concealed carry licenses, often requiring that the applicant prove to the authority's satisfaction that they "needed" to carry a gun. The abuses were blatant, like the situation cited by Cramer who writes, "In the City of Los Angeles, the police administration refused to issue any permits at all. In a city of over three million people, from 1984 until 1992, not one person was found by the Los Angeles Police Department to 'need' a handgun permit."[3]

In 1987, a crime-oppressed population in Florida organized and pushed through reasonable legislation allowing Floridians to carry concealed handguns to protect themselves. Prior to 1987, Florida chief law enforcement officers held complete discretion over approving concealed carry license applications, with the result that few licenses were issued. The 1987 legislative victory to require approval of applications, unless the applicant was disqualified by a specific list of factors including criminal history, inspired many similar efforts all across the nation. Florida became an early tile in a domino effect that has changed concealed carry rights in most of the United States.

At the time this book was written, only eight states cling to the "may-issue" model. Shall-issue policies are now the norm. On the extreme ends of the spectrum, as of this writing only Illinois continues to fight legislation to legalize concealed carry, and at the other extreme, a small number of states allow unrestricted carry, requiring no state-issued license at all, which is sometimes jubilantly called "Constitutional carry." This is the practice in Alabama, Arizona, Vermont, outside city limits in Montana, and is legal for Wyoming residents, although non-residents may not carry in the Cowboy state without a license.

A PATCHWORK OF LAWS

Laws governing carrying concealed weapons have little uniformity from one state to another, since most applicable gun possession laws are under the purview of each state, not beneath the thumb of the federal government. Worse, inside some states, armed citizens labor under a patchwork of laws that make it difficult to know if it is legal to carry from one county to the next or inside one city or another. It makes obeying gun laws nearly impossible! To avoid that, a goodly number of state legislatures have implemented the concept of pre-emption, by which the state's gun laws decree that the state is the controlling authority on any gun laws. Any municipal or county laws that are more restrictive than those enacted by the state are thereby invalid. Pre-emption is a good thing! Read your state laws to find out if it is in effect where you live.

Carry into illegal areas figures prominently in reasons licensing authorities cite for revoking citizens' licenses to carry.

Even where pre-emption is the rule and licensed concealed carry a normal practice, there are still a number of restrictions that prevent the concealed carry licensee from taking their handgun into any of the so-called gun-free zones. The best well-known restricted areas are schools in most states and beyond the security check point of airports. A number of airports are now posted as entirely gun-free zones, which may or may not be enforceable in light of pre-emption laws in force in a lot of states. Federal facilities like courts, post offices and military bases have long led the list of federal facilities on to which a licensee may not carry a gun. Until a 2010, National Parks were included in the list of prohibited areas. Now only the buildings, like visitor centers or administrative facilities in National Parks, remain off-limits to the citizen who can legally carry a gun in the state in which the park is located, considerably easing the burden on licensed armed citizens who hike, camp and drive through our National Parks.

Most states also restrict firearms possession inside courthouses, mental hospitals, police stations, jails, sometimes in schools, churches and bars, on public transit like city busses and regional transit trains, and private property owners are almost always allowed to prohibit gun possession on their property, if that is their desire. A notable exception has been victories won by gun rights activists through which employees in a number of states now enjoy the right to secure a gun in their automobile in the company parking lot even if required to go into the work place disarmed. Of course, none of the state-level gun restrictions are uniform nationwide, so you must study your state's laws carefully.

A thorough understanding of state and federal law about concealed carry restrictions is essential. Statistics about concealed carry license revocations show that carry into illegal areas figures prominently in reasons licensing authorities cite for revoking citizens' licenses to carry. In addition to specific venues into which it is illegal to take a handgun, most states have restrictions on licensed carry if the citizen is intoxicated, and conviction for a felony or misdemeanor crime is also grounds upon which states revoke concealed carry licenses.

> *Some armed citizens, having completed an elementary licensing course, do not realize how very cursory that training is.*

Unlike a driving license, a license to carry a concealed handgun is primarily recognized by the issuing state only, though the concept of license reciprocity has been gaining popularity. Sometimes neighboring states will honor one another's concealed carry licenses, and more commonly, states will forge reciprocity agreements with other states that enforce similar standards and requirements for concealed carry licensing. Among the most prominent, concealed carry licenses from Utah and Florida have the greatest numbers of other states that recognize and honor their license, though several others come close.

When depending on reciprocity to legally carry concealed, you will need to understand and obey the laws in the reciprocating states. Reciprocal license recognition can change on the whim of a state's legislature or a state's attorney general. A common encroachment comes from states that declared they would give reciprocal recognition to the Utah or Florida permit, for example, but only to residents of Utah or Florida (the issuing states). Thus, for example, a Californian who was traveling in Colorado, expecting their Utah permit would be honored, was in for an awful surprise when it turned out that while Colorado ostensibly granted reciprocity to Utah's permit, that favor was actually only extended to Utah residents.

Gary Slider's website www.handgunlaw.us is currently the best resource for verifying reciprocity. If you are traveling, it doesn't take long to map your route to identify which states you will pass through, then go to the handgunlaw.us website and print out the gun law information for those states. Not only does Slider's website give you good reference materials, carrying printed copies of the law citations might provide the state code showing your behavior is legal, if challenged en route by a poorly-informed representative of the law, though one should engage in such an argument only with the greatest of courtesy and caution.

More than half of the state laws providing for concealed carry licensure of qualified citizens require the applicant to show proof of training and proficiency. The training required varies from state-mandated courses to gun safety programs certified by the National Rifle Association. The shooting proficiency tests tend to be relatively elementary. Still, these requirements imbue the licensing process with a legitimacy that seems to comfort the lawmakers. Required training classes and the shooting proficiency tests are generally administered by private businesses that charge for the service, adding to the expense of obtaining a license to carry.

Training requirements create two disadvantages: the prices charged can put access to concealed carry licensing out of reach for ordinary citizens, and some armed citizens, having completed an elementary licensing course, do not realize how very cursory that training is for a woman or man who may carry a handgun into a variety of challenging circumstances that require a far higher level of skill. On the other hand, training requirements introduce the new licensee to training organizations, and so I hope that if you live in a state with a training requirement that you will use the mandatory training as a jumping off place from which to pursue further education to increase accuracy and gun manipulation skills, and to begin to study strategies and tactics to prevail against a variety of attacks.

We've outlined a lot of requirements to which the licensed citizen carrying a concealed handgun must comply. In addition to careful study of your state's website to learn about state gun laws, taking an active interest in ongoing firearms training is a good way to stay up to date on current laws. Let your licensing class be just the first, exciting step on a lifetime practice of training and skill development.

---

(1) www.claytoncramer.com/popular/duelinganddeliverance.pdf

(2) Assembly Bill 263 (Hawes – 1923) Chapter 339, Statutes of 1923 regulating "a) the manufacture and sale of dangerous weapons, b) providing for registration of weapons, c) prohibiting carrying of concealed firearms except when lawfully authorized; d) providing for confiscation and destruction of weapons; e) prohibiting ownership by certain classes of persons, and f) prescribing penalties for violation of the provisions of the Act.

(3) http://www.claytoncramer.com/scholarly/shall-issue.html

INTERACTIONS WITH THE CRIMINAL JUSTICE SYSTEM

Have you thought about interacting with law enforcement officers during traffic stops while you are carrying? Have you considered how or whether you should announce you are carrying a gun if an officer conducts a field interview with you? Do you know how to go armed in public in ways that do not alarm the unarmed citizenry, so they don't call the police to report a hazard? What happens if you have to draw your concealed handgun to prevent an assault? What happens if you have to shoot in self defense? Interaction with police and the legal system is unavoidable after self defense, but it will be easier if you have an idea what to expect and know what is expected of you. This chapter will shine the light of reality on some of those concerns.

As we discussed in the previous chapter, carrying a concealed handgun is legal throughout most of America, so long as the armed citizen obtains the state-issued license where required, knows the controlling law, pays attention to specific locations that remain off-limits even to licensed handgun carry, and respects other state and federal laws as applicable. In short, there is nothing sneaky or illicit about concealed handgun carry, despite the uneasiness expressed by many who carry concealed. This apprehension is most often voiced by armed citizens within their first few years of practicing concealed carry, though a realistic concern about alarming the anti-gun public by unintentionally revealing a concealed handgun remains understandably strong among citizens living in anti-gun environments.

One of the primary fears expressed is that the armed citizen will be detained or their right to carry a personal protection handgun will be challenged by police. Unspecified fears about interacting with police stem from the natural human terror at loss of control over one's destiny and so, instead of viewing law enforcement as a neutral force in the law-abiding citizen's life, suspicion, mistrust and even animosity blossom. In my experience, in locales in which it is legal to carry a concealed handgun, most uniformed patrol officers understand that the practice is lawful and are primarily concerned that armed citizens carry safely and do not bring out their guns in public. In other words—don't ask, don't tell, and certainly do not show!

The laws in some states require the armed citizen who is contacted by a police officer to declare if they are carrying a gun, as is the case in Ohio, Michigan and Kansas, to name only a few. While these requirements are the exception, not the standard, knowing how to inform law enforcement that you are carrying, without alarming the officer, is essential. The smartest choice of words may be, for example, "I have a Kansas license to carry a concealed handgun and the gun is on my right hip, sir/ma'am. How would you prefer to proceed?" There is no need to apologize or to be defensive – just state the conditions as required by law and then follow the officer's directions, which will probably either be not to touch or handle the gun, or to surrender the gun to the officer for the duration of the police contact. It would, of course, be very unwise to start this conversation by blurting, "I have a gun!" And yet, without having thought about how you will fulfill this requirement of the law, it is hard to guess what words might come out of your mouth, since for most a traffic stop or other police contact is stressful owing to the unfamiliarity of the experience.

In states that do not require the armed citizen to declare if they are carrying a gun, I believe it is wiser to behave discreetly, comply with requests the officer makes, and only mention the gun if the officer is likely to come in contact with the gun. For example, if you are asked to step out of your car, the officer may do a cursory search in the name of officer safety or discover the gun another way, while administering a field sobriety test, for example. When that is likely, it is only sensible to explain about your carry license and ask for direction in advance.

> *Knowing how to inform law enforcement that you are carrying, without alarming the officer, is essential.*

Increasing computerization may provide the officer stopping you with information about your carry license and display your licensing details on the patrol car's mobile data terminal when they run your car's registration and license through the state's database. Sometimes officers will ask if you have weapons in your car, either based on that information or as a routine inquiry he or she habitually makes to increase officer safety, whether they think you have a gun or not. You know from the earlier paragraphs how to handle these questions, and certainly should not try to hide it if you are carrying your self-defense gun.

These are only a few examples of why thorough knowledge of both state and municipal law affecting concealed carry where you are is critical. Fortunately, there are a number of online resources plus many printed law guides, and either an online search or buying an up-to-date copy of a gun laws book that covers your state is, in my opinion, obligatory for everyone who carries a gun. One of the best resources for gun law books for the various states is Alan Korwin's Bloomfield Press (www.gunlaws.com) or you could ask for resource suggestions from your local gun rights lobbying group, since they probably know and work with the law expert in your state and have a vested interest in helping armed citizens stay on the right side of the law. In addition, you need to invest the time to fully read, study and understand your state's laws on firearms and on justifiable use of defensive force, starting with an online search of your state's website. If you don't have Internet access or if you find research challenging, ask for help at your local library.

THE ARMED CITIZEN AND
THE CRIMINAL JUSTICE SYSTEM

Usually when law enforcement interacts with someone with a gun, the person with a gun is a suspect who has committed a crime, often assault and sometimes life has been taken. The default operating procedure, then, is that the person with the gun needs to be secured and separated from the firearm until police can determine if they committed a crime. A range of defensive acts – from simply putting your hand on the grips of your gun and giving verbal orders to leave you alone, to pointing a gun at an assailant but not shooting, all the way up to the very serious necessity of shooting an assailant – all contain the elements of varying degrees of the crime of assault, sometimes codified as first degree assault, second degree assault and so on. The law is not initially concerned with *justification* for these actions. The law is only interested in whether or not your actions fulfill the elements of the crimes of menacing, simple assault, battery, assault with a deadly weapon or, as defined in many states, the various degrees of assault. Many people who are new to guns for self defense are alarmed to learn that self-defense actions contain the elements of these crimes.

Only a thorough investigation makes clear the justification for using deadly force in self defense, so that the criminal justice system can put the criminal in prison and release the person who was forced to act in self defense. In early phases of interaction with law enforcement, the armed citizen may feel that they are accused, badgered and mistreated, depending on the methods the investigator uses to ferret out the truth of what actually happened.

If the justifiability of the armed citizens' self-defense use of their firearm is not readily apparent, law enforcement may forward the case to the district attorney (DA) or prosecutor who must analyze the facts of the incident, relying on law enforcement reports, then decide if the armed citizen committed a crime or if the state law allows their actions by reason of self defense. The next step varies from state to state, with some using a Grand Jury to decide if probable cause that a crime was committed is strong enough to indict or bring charges against the accused; other states leave that determination in the hands of the District Attorney. If indicted, the citizen is given a hearing in front of a judge at which time a plea of guilty or not guilty is entered; bail and other pre-trial details are also decided in hearings prior to the trial.

Realizing that actions taken with a concealed handgun carried for self defense can result in becoming the defendant in a courtroom is a sobering revelation for many new gun owners. Understanding what the law allows, and how the criminal justice system will determine if you've acted in compliance with the law, as outlined briefly above, is essential before exercising the right to armed self defense. Before moving on to topics specific to guns, holsters and concealment, let's close with a brief discussion of when it is justifiable to use your gun in self defense.

WHAT THE LAW ALLOWS

Though couched in various terms in the different state penal codes, the law essentially allows an innocent person to use deadly force to defend against an immediate danger of death or disabling injury that the intended victim cannot avoid. There are a lot of complex elements to that overly simplified definition, so let's break it down.

Deadly force is any means through which life is put at risk. Armed citizens tend to think of deadly force as only applying to their guns, but deadly force can be exerted with bare hands, knives and any number of every-day things, including heavy objects, power tools or your automobile! Deadly force may only be justifiably used in defense if the threat is likely to cause your death or serious, disabling injury. It is not an appropriate response to property crimes, many forms of harassment, verbal confrontations or other general nastiness that comes your way as part of daily life.

The question of preclusion or avoiding situations that result in using a gun in self defense is widely argued, with various Stand Your Ground laws recognizing that it is unreasonably dangerous to require citizens to retreat from an in-progress attack. In addition to understanding your own state's law, it is also valuable to understand that criminal charges and court decisions hinge on a preponderance of the evidence, and if the facts show that you tried to avoid, stop or deescalate the dangerous situation, you will have a much stronger position from which to argue that you were backed into a corner until you had little choice but to defend yourself.

It would be foolish to discuss justifiable use of deadly force in self defense without acknowledging the enormous contributions to our knowledge coming from Massad Ayoob,[1] author of *In the Gravest Extreme*, the *Gun Digest Book of Concealed Carry*, *Gun Digest Book of Combat Handgunnery* and dozens of other books and recorded lectures on DVD. Ayoob was among the first to define and teach the justifiability of use of the firearm in the defense of the private citizen. His teachings continue to be available through Massad Ayoob Group classes, as well as books, magazine articles and DVDs that he has authored.

If you carry a gun for self defense or plan to do so, do not fail to pursue a full understanding of when, why, how and what you are allowed to do in self defense, as well as regularly updating your knowledge. Few instructors teach this subject as clearly as does Ayoob, and as his website at www.massadayoobgroup. com shows, he travels all across the United States teaching seminars and shooting courses. If you have the opportunity to learn from this preeminent leader in the field, do not miss it.

Too many armed citizens assert that they'll "know" when the threat of death or injury is sufficiently serious to warrant using their gun. That's a little like saying that a new driver will instinctively know when to brake hard or when to accelerate to drive through a dangerous situation. To access the right solution during an emergency, the information on which to base the correct decision has to already be pre-loaded into the computer of your mind. Only training, study and soul-searching prepares the armed citizen to deal with using deadly force against another human to preserve your own life or that of another innocent person.

Concerns about justifiable use of force include perceiving when the danger is so serious that no other viable survival options exist below introducing a gun into the situation. Ayoob teaches that unless a triad of factors is present in the situation, deadly force is not warranted. These factors are ability, opportunity and jeopardy. Ability means that the assailant has the means with which to inflict great bodily harm on you or another innocent person. Opportunity means that they are within range to make effective use of whatever weapon or means they have of inflicting harm. Jeopardy means that the assailant is acting in a way that a reasonable and prudent person would recognize that they intended to inflict crippling injury or kill right then and there. When a judge or jury is asked to decide if an armed citizen behaved within the constraints of the law in defending herself or himself, the trier of fact is asked to decide what a reasonable and prudent person knowing what the citizen knew at the time of the incident would have done. Prescience is not required, but neither is acting recklessly in a blind panic accepted.

This short introduction to use of deadly force in self defense is a little like reading the introductory chapter of a textbook about a complex subject like physiology. There is a lot more to it. And unlike most textbook subject matter, failing to understand when you're allowed to use deadly force against another human being has serious, life-altering consequences! For a start, obtain the booklet *What Every Gun Owner Needs to Know About Self-Defense Law*, published by the Armed Citizens' Legal Defense Network, Inc. It is available as a download at the website www.armedcitizensnetwork.org. By way of full disclosure, the Network is an armed citizens' legal resource I helped establish in 2008. Other study resources include Massad Ayoob's books, including his book *In the Gravest Extreme* as well as his lecture on DVD entitled *Judicious Use of Deadly Force*. Though much of Marc MacYoung's writings deal with physical self defense or martial arts, his website at http://www.nononsenseselfdefense.com/lethalforce.html is also a rich resource that will keep you reading for many hours.

Understanding the law about when you can use a gun in self defense is every bit as important as understanding the law that allows you to carry that gun. While legalities are not the topic of this book, the effort of understanding the fine points of the law, and of interacting with law enforcement and the courts in the aftermath of a self-defense shooting, are important components in deciding if carrying a handgun for personal protection is a responsibility you are prepared to shoulder. The consequences of using a gun in self defense are so serious and long-lasting that you owe it to yourself and others to fully understand the justifiability of use of force before you are in a position to use a gun in self defense.

---

(1) Massad Ayoob Group, P. O. Box 1477, Live Oak, FL 32064, www.massadayoobgroup.com

INTERACTIONS WITH SOCIETY: ETIQUETTE FOR ARMED WOMEN

The responsible armed citizen's comportment goes far toward avoiding catastrophes like discoveries by horrified employers and business associates, distant relatives and casual acquaintances who shriek, "Are you carrying a gun? Today?"

Carrying a self-defense gun brings with it a lot of responsibilities. The greatest duty, without doubt, is to understand the legal constraints on concealed carry and the laws bearing on use of deadly force in self defense. Next, it is essential that we practice scrupulously safe procedures for using firearms, so that we do not irresponsibly harm others or ourselves. Armed citizens shoulder another uncodified but very real social responsibility, and that is to respect those members of society in whom an unreasoning fear of guns has been instilled.

Respect does not mean sacrificing our means of self defense to allay the anti-gun terrors that are very real to people who hate or fear guns. I believe respect means finding ways to take care of your own defense needs without impinging on these fearful folks' entitlement to sustain their own variety of comfort, even if it is wildly at odds with your worldview. In short, our responsibility to others means knowing when it is acceptable to talk about your gun or to allow your gun to be seen, and avoiding doing so when it creates unease or fear. Besides, there are a lot of very valid reasons to keep your self-defense gun your own secret.

HUSH...DON'T SAY A WORD!

Silence is golden, and keeping quiet has special value to the woman who carries a concealed handgun. Despite the feminine tendency to talk things out, a characteristic called "external information processing," the decision to carry a gun for self defense is one choice about which you must exercise extreme discretion in word and action. Women often discuss personal decisions with a wide variety of friends, casual acquaintances and sometimes even with strangers. It is a way of seeking validation, especially for decisions that we fear others may judge harshly. Perhaps we hope our fears of disapproval will be disproven, so we lay out our secrets for all to see, hoping someone will soothe us with kind words, "It's OK, dear…" Unfortunately, there are people who so hate and fear guns that they cannot separate your many good characteristics from the gun you carry, because firearms are objects for which they harbor so much fear and hatred.

Even if the person to whom you talked about carrying a gun holds neutral opinions on gun rights, have you considered to whom she may gossip? A team member at work? A supervisor or employer? A social contact that could open doors for you? Someone at your church? A leader where you volunteer? There is no reason to jeopardize your advancement for the momentary balm of another person's understanding. Self reliance and personal protection do not enjoy wide-spread popularity, and your present and future associates may not share your commitment to those principles. Why jeopardize your individual advancement?

There are other reasons why disclosing that you carry a gun is a bad idea. When people are new to guns for self defense, a lot of self-examination is natural. We ask, "What is right, moral and ethical?" Perhaps we should ask, "What is smart?" The prominence of attitudes that denigrate self-reliance makes it very likely that some people to whom you reveal that you carry a concealed handgun will tell you in no uncertain terms and with the utter confidence of blind belief that a woman with a gun is likely to be disarmed and killed

Do not confuse telling all your secrets with bonding.

with her own gun; that what you are doing is illegal and you will be arrested; that you are crazy, paranoid, or harbor a secret desire to kill someone; and even more far-fetched assertions. These anti-gun arguments end with the unstated presumption that the speaker fears and hates guns, and by extension he or she may have to think long and hard about liking you! The message implies, "Why don't you just be more normal and get rid of that scary gun?"

Instead of suggestions that instill self-doubt, most women need ideas and affirmations that encourage individual confidence. Talking about guns for self defense with people who do not share your commitment to self sufficiency is all too likely to produce thoughts and fears that feed self doubt. Women who are taking on new challenges simply do not need this kind of sabotage.

Do not confuse telling all your secrets with bonding. That's a common lie promoted by the culture of a society that is driven to thwart individual initiative.

WHO TO TELL

Who needs to know that you carry a gun? The list is surprisingly short. Someone once said you should only speak of carrying a gun with people with whom you are comfortable being naked, and I had to smile since there was a fair bit of common sense in the picturesque idea. Naturally, it makes sense to talk about going armed with anyone who will have such close physical contact with you that they will see or feel your holstered gun. If you practice good conceal-ment, that limits disclosure to a surprisingly short list of close intimates, like your spouse or live-in significant other, but actually may or may not include your parents, or your offspring, depending on your stage of life and depending on their ability to keep your secret.

Does not telling family that you have become an armed citizen seem impossible? You'd be surprised how closely you can interact with people and avoid discovery of your choice to carry a concealed handgun. Do your family members and other close associates embrace one another often? Keeping your gun secret while hugging and being hugged is not as big a problem as you might think.

When contact may bring someone close to your holstered gun, drop your arm over it to block contact with it from the other's hip, arm, or other incoming body part. Hugs require the same strategy. Take a hint from a good friend of mine who explained how to cope with the hugs at AA meetings: when embracing, one person's arm has to be on top, so the armed citizen lets the other person take the "high" position. If you embrace the other person from beneath their arms, your arm is always between them and your gun. No one is the wiser, and more importantly, you don't have to squirm around and act like you are hiding something.

If you are with your child or an intimate who knows that you carry a gun, they can also provide a buffer zone in crowded environments by walking or sitting on the same side as your gun is carried, though they need to learn in an emergency to run away or get behind you and not to cling to the hand or arm you would use to draw. In addition, it is only sensible to coach these intimates about the dangers of revealing to others that you carry a gun, whether that is in conversation or during a tense confrontation. As the responsible armed citizen, you must be the one who decides if efforts to deescalate have failed and introducing your gun into the situation is the only viable option remaining.

Under circumstances where revealing that you carry a personal protection handgun will not advance your cause, you really can live quite happily keeping your gun ownership beneath the radar. Humans want attention for a variety of reasons, though most often that seems to be associated with the pursuit of romance! Understand that when, by appearance or action, you go all-out to attract attention, you will get attention from as many or more undesirable people than from folks with whom you would like to connect. The less general attention you attract, the less likely it is that anyone will notice your concealed carry handgun. Going armed is best practiced only by emotionally mature people. Folks who need a lot of attention may find that carrying a concealed handgun is not their best mode of personal protection.

You read that right – there really are people for whom carrying a concealed handgun is a dreadfully inappropriate self-defense choice. That in no way reflects on their value to humanity or upon the contributions that they make. If one's level of personal accountability is diminished by lifestyle or temperament, carrying a gun is not for them, because responsibly carrying a gun requires an extremely high degree of individual responsibility. Drunkenness or recreational drug use, for example, have no place in the life of the armed citizen. Making excuses instead of getting training to develop shooting proficiency is another form of irresponsibility. These failings create problems for the larger community of legitimate gun owners, and for that reason, if you can't carry a concealed handgun responsibly, please work out non-firearms self-defense provisions.

The individual whose arms embrace above the other's shoulders need never come in contact with a belt-holstered gun, because the armed citizen's elbow can keep their arms high or lower them if needed cover the gun and keep it out of reach of the person they are embracing.
Photo by John Hall

LEAKS WILL HAPPEN

If the word gets out that you carry a defense gun, you will inevitably face the inappropriately curious question, "Do you really carry a gun? Are you doing that right now?" If a firm denial isn't appropriate, my favorite solution is a vague response, "I carry when it is appropriate, that's all. No big deal. Hey, I heard you just got back from a vacation to Belize! That sounds wonderful..." Smoothly guide the conversation to focus on the other person and engage that irrepressible human love of talking about oneself while drawing attention away from the impending inappropriate discussion about you!

Intimates, close family members, your children and others who know that you carry a gun need to be briefed about your role as an armed citizen in an unsafe world. If you witness a risky situation from which you have decided to quietly withdraw, the last thing you need is an associate who loudly proclaims, "Get out your gun, Mary, that [expletive deleted] has a knife!" Since you cannot control another person's panicked response, it is simply better to limit these accidental exposures by keeping to yourself knowledge of the gun you carry for personal protection.

Children, too, need to understand that telling others private information from inside the family can have dire consequences. Just as children must learn at an early age not to reveal things like where the family hides the extra key to the house, when you are leaving on vacation, or other private details, the children of armed citizens must be made to understand the grave consequences of revealing that adult household members have guns.

Resolve to keep private your decision to carry a gun for personal protection. Learn to smile at everyone, avoid acting furtively, and still remain ready to defend yourself if someone you thought was harmless does not turn out to be safe. You may very well become the determined individual who has to defend yourself or innocent people you care about from a predator who wants to victimize, rape, assault or kill.

That is the reason we carry guns for self defense and we need to keep that mission foremost in our minds. We don't carry guns so we can feel invulnerable, or so that we can get away with behaving aggressively or foolishly. We don't brag about being able to take risks because we carry a gun. None of that is useful or wise. We carry a gun because we know that predators exist and we simply take precautions to avoid becoming prey.

JUST LEARNING TO SHOOT?

Carrying a gun is not a smart defense choice if you lack the skills to make the necessary shot in an emergency. A tool without a skilled operator is all but useless, and worse, it may be dangerous. This chapter is a discussion of reasonable standards for shooting skills, how to improve your marksmanship and how to maintain your defensive edge.

Errors while drawing and holstering a handgun account for some of the most common and most dangerous safety violations armed citizens make with their handguns. Thus, before we can learn the safe and effective use of concealment holsters, we must thoroughly master gun safety, including no-compromise safety when putting the gun in the holster and drawing it, too.

The first challenge of gun safety is to cement in place a habit of never doing anything with any firearm–loaded or unloaded–that could cause injury yourself or another innocent person. That's a surprisingly high standard, since the self-defense usefulness of a handgun is the direct result of a gun's ability to inflict devastating physical harm. Gun safety starts with stringent control of where the muzzle of the firearm points at all times. Before even picking up and handling a gun, it is essential to select a safe direction in which to point it, including making sure that the path the muzzle travels on its way to point into that safe direction does not contain anything you are not willing to shoot. If the muzzle will cross someone or something the gun would injure if discharged, stop before you pick up the gun and figure out a different, safer way to move it.

What makes a safe direction into which to point a gun? Anything that would stop the bullet from the most powerful cartridge the gun can discharge. Bear in mind that most handgun ammunition can penetrate interior and often exterior walls in modern housing, as well as the floors between upper and lower stories in many buildings. In the home, a safe gun handling location might include a fireplace made of solid river rock, a long and tightly packed shelf of large books, and one of the professional bullet-resistant products like those sold by Safe Direction[1] or a panel from a surplus bullet-resistant vest. Probably the cleverest solution I ever saw came from my friend Kathy Jackson, who went

Women at the Firearms Academy of Seattle, Inc. study penetration potential for various calibers of ammunition when shot through a section of ordinary housing construction—sheetrock, studs, insulation and exterior cladding. Even tiny .22LR bullets went through to put a slowly leaking hole into a plastic bottle of colored water. The .357 Magnum shown here caused quite a splash.

on to become the founder of the Cornered Cat Training Company.[2] For one of our women's programs on safe backstops, she showed the audience how to fill a large, approximately twenty gallon planter with fine sand, pretty it up with silk foliage, and use it as a safe backstop for loading and unloading inside the home, much as police departments, armorers and gun stores have provided unloading barrels for decades.

Why does muzzle direction matter when the gun is unloaded? Safe muzzle direction is of great import because any time a gun is in your hands you are cementing habits that influence what you will do with a gun when your attention is fragmented, as it certainly is during a self-defense emergency. It matters because gun accidents happen when people mindlessly assume the gun is unloaded. You must take safe muzzle direction very seriously.

Absent a mechanical malfunction, a gun does not discharge unless rearward pressure is applied to the trigger. Thus, when someone unintentionally fires a gun, it is usually because they put their finger on the trigger. Until a conscious decision to fire has been made and the gun is pointed at the target,

Safe Direction Academy Pad [1] ballistic containment panel provides safe bullet-catching backstop in any environment, be that an apartment building, motel room, or anywhere else you need to safely handle guns that lacks a bullet-stopping backstop.

your finger must remain off the trigger to assure you do not inadvertently press it, either through inattention or an involuntary contraction of the hand, such as occurs when you lose your balance or are startled.

Indexing your finger off the trigger and outside the trigger guard is usually the most difficult safety practice for beginners to make into a habit, owing to the shape and design of the gun, which encourages putting the finger on the trigger. The coaching and correction you'll receive in a beginning firearms class will introduce the habit of indexing your trigger finger up on the frame of the gun above the trigger guard until you point the gun at the target and you have decided to shoot. After class is over, you must continue to vigilantly practice this safety habit anytime you hold a gun. Safety doesn't "just happen," it is the result of careful attention to detail. Rarely do accidents "just happen," either. When someone is inadvertently injured, inattention to safety is consistently the cause. No matter how viable the excuse for violating the safety rules sounds, the injury or loss from unintentionally discharging a firearm can be permanent and unrecoverable. Gun safety is a very serious and vital subject.

Because we are discussing handguns carried for self defense, we need to also be concerned with discharging a handgun in the safest way possible. There are a variety of handgun operating systems, and learning to safely operate the

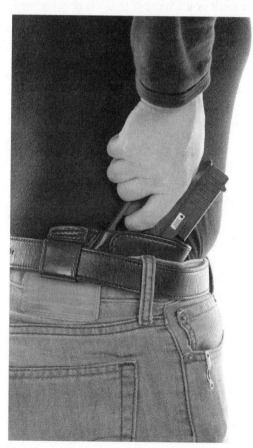

one you choose to carry is one of the most important reasons you must take firearms classes. Beyond safe and efficient handgun operation, accurately shooting in self defense without injuring innocent bystanders at the incident is of equal concern.

Consider the August 2012 police shooting in crowded New York City. While murderer Jeffrey T. Johnson was shot and killed, three uninvolved citizens who had the misfortune to be in crowded mid-town Manhattan that morning were injured, and a half dozen others hurt by ricochets of bullets that did not hit Johnson,

Don't do this! Keep your finger off the trigger and outside of the trigger guard until the gun is pointed at the target and you have decided to shoot! This illustration, made with an inert Ring's Blue Gun, demonstrates how the holster presses into a finger left on the trigger, showing why this gun safety rule is so very important to the discussion of carrying handguns for self defense.

as well as debris launched when bullets that missed hit and shattered concrete and other building surface materials. Armed self defense in a crowded environment requires high levels of skill. This is a realistic concern, because the threats against which we carry guns can and often do occur in crowded areas.

Many armed citizens wondered what they would have done had they been in the Aurora, CO, theater July 20, 2012, when James Holmes shot and killed a dozen people and injured nearly 60 others. To have shot only Holmes in the reduced lighting, crowded conditions and around the protective gear Holmes wore would have demanded very skilled marksmanship.

You may have been told that private citizens don't have to train to shoot accurately at distances beyond arm's reach. How could anyone who reads the news believe that? You cannot predict what violence you may be swept up in and, although you are unwillingly drawn into the conflict, you remain responsible for all

> **You remain responsible for all the shots you fire, not just the shots that hit the assailant.**

the shots you fire, not just the shots that hit the assailant. If you carry a gun for self defense, you must train and practice until you have strong skills that include safe gun handling as well as shooting accuracy.

Accurate shooting is based on a small set of foundational skills, on which more complicated defensive skills, like speed shooting, low light shooting or shooting a moving assailant, are dependent. With that in mind, let's outline the fundamental skills in play when the trigger pull results in a center-target hit.

Many instructional programs begin with aiming the gun, and we will get to aiming in good time, but I think that by first focusing on traditional sighting methods, the new student may fail to grasp how much trigger control affects accurate shooting. While the handgun and ammunition have some influence on accuracy, most inaccurate shots can be attributed to incorrect trigger manipulation that jerks the muzzle off target the instant before and while the shot is discharging.

You see, the most common and possibly most challenging shooter's error is the flinching reaction caused by the shooter's anticipation of the noise and recoil that occurs when the gun discharges. Curing a flinch requires overriding the human startle reflex that is integral to our innate survival system. Defeating a shooter's flinch is accomplished through a variety of training exercises that acclimate the shooter to the noise and movement of a discharging firearm, as well as managing the mental aspect of shooting to focus attention entirely on smoothly applying pressure to and then resetting the trigger, not on predicting the moment at which the gun will fire. A skilled and intuitive shooting coach is a tremendous resource when the student must learn to overcome the flinch, as well as develop related trigger control skills.

Aiming a handgun is a multi-faceted aspect of accurate shooting. At its most fundamental, aiming with the pistol sights (called "getting a sight picture" or "aligning the sights") involves positioning the front sight so it is viewed through the notch of the rear sight such that the top of the front sight is no higher or lower than the tops of the rear sight, and equal space (often described as light) is visible on either side of the front sight as it is framed on the left and the right by the rear sight.

This view of the sights is laid over the target, with the front sight covering the location on the target that the shooter wishes to hit.

This sight use, called a combat sight picture, differs from what is called a target sighting arrangement, in which the top of the front sight is held right at the bottom of the bulls eye the shooter wishes to hit. Target sight use is dependent on distance, though, and with that variable unpredictable in self defense shooting, it is not useful for self defense pistol accuracy, though you may see it illustrated in training guidebooks and in the owner's manual that came with your handgun.

Most shooters will learn to primarily aim with their dominant eye focused to see the front sight sharply enough to determine that it is correctly centered in the notch of the rear sight. Are you having trouble lining up pistol sights when the sights are blurry or appear to move around? Sight alignment is not a lot different than the tight visual focus required to thread a needle. Well, what do you do when you can't tell if you are getting the thread close to the eye of the needle? You close an eye. You do it automatically. No one needs to tell you that you need to close your non-dominant eye to see the needle and thread more clearly. You just close an eye, and the dominant eye takes over and gives you the view needed to insert that pesky thread into the tiny eye of the needle. However, beginning handgun training usually includes instruction in identifying the dominant eye.

Depending on lighting, visual acuity, and the color and size of the sights, attaining a sight picture can sometimes be all but impossible. Shooters often squint the non-dominant eye to help the stronger eye focus clearly on the pistol's front

sight, flanked by the posts of the rear sight, which will appear slightly blurry. The applicability of this practice to shooting while under attack is dubious, yet you will see it done on the practice and training range, and we should not ignore any method that helps make a demanding shot more accurate, since it is not possible to predict the exact circumstances in which a defensive handgun may be needed. The difficulty of using a precision sight picture during exigent circumstances leads us to alternative sighting methods, which have much to contribute to accurate shooting under bad conditions.

Additional sighting methods attempt to provide more practical aiming techniques in close-and-fast emergency

When the sights are aligned over a target, we call the view a sight picture, as in, "Did you see a sight picture as you fired?"

conditions that may include moving while shooting, shooting to hit a moving assailant, shooting in low light and other conditions that make it hard to maintain sight alignment or clearly focus on the sights.

Sighting variations include looking over the sights during close-in speed shooting, defined by master instructor Massad Ayoob as StressPoint Index and sometimes called "shooting out of the notch" by competitive shooters. Proponents of this sighting method explain that while the handgun is actually aligned on the target, the shooter has not taken time to lower her head to peer through the rear sight to see the traditional sight alignment. From the shooter's viewpoint, the front sight appears higher than the rear sight, though in actuality that is a visual distortion. This coarse alignment of the sights usually yields acceptable accuracy as far out as ten to twelve yards, and the technique is much quicker to use than traditional sight alignment because the eyes need index only on the front sight as it overlays the target.

StressPoint Index sight use is quick to attain because the eye need only focus on the front sight seen above the slide and rear sight, and indexed on the center of the target.

An even coarser aiming method simply overlays the entire silhouette of the handgun over a close target, since if the assailant is so near that the outline of his chest and shoulders is not blocked out by the larger-appearing handgun, shots fired hit the center chest area if the shooter practices good trigger control. Because there is less involved, this aiming method is very fast. It may be best remembered as "Weapon Silhouette" by handgunning students fortunate enough to study with Jim Cirillo while he was alive.

Famous police and Special Forces small arms instructor Ken Hackathorn teaches that it is unrealistic to expect a person to attempt any skill in an emergency that has not been honed to a high degree of comfort and confidence through training and practice. He's right! Don't expect to be ready to use any handgun sighting method without practicing until you know you can hit ac-

Jim Cirillo's weapon silhouette is applicable to large, close targets, as would be the case if attacked at close range, circumstances under which the silhouette of the gun would appear surrounded by the outline of the assailant's torso in the intended victim's field of view.

curately every time you use it. Since a beginning handgunning class puts the most if not all the emphasis on traditional sight use, intermediate and advanced shooting skills training is important when you carry a handgun for self defense so you can learn and integrate these more advanced skills.

The handguns of the 21st century are considerably more refined than the earliest pistols, but they still have front sights and rear sights and our use of pistol sights remains fundamentally unchanged from the 1800s. One useful accessory that augments but does not replace traditional sights is the sighting laser. Laser sights are made by a variety of manufacturers who sell housings that include a laser diode, a power source and the circuitry to control the laser beam so that, when mounted on a handgun and properly adjusted, it projects a dot of light onto the target at the same place a fired round will strike. Laser sights don't replace pistol sights, but under some conditions lasers can provide an extremely useful alternative, so military and law enforcement personnel as well as armed citizens find they are worth the expense.

Benjamin Franklin identified humans as the "tool-making animal," and in

LEFT: [Left to right] Comparing replica Colt Single-Action Army revolver, modern Smith & Wesson Model 686 and Smith & Wesson 3rd Model single-action revolver shows how modern revolver sights, center, are much easier to see.

ABOVE & RIGHT: This antique pistol's front and rear sights are very small.

light of our love of machines, gadgets and devices, it is pretty clear that he was right. Armed citizens demonstrate this proclivity by buying numerous guns, hoping all the while that each new pistol will improve their shooting abilities and all the while ignoring their need for training and practice. Of course, that doesn't work for the armed citizen any better than buying a fast, new car makes an inexperienced driver more skillful. And, like driving, the gun owner needs not only basic skills and advanced skills, but also needs to refine and maintain those skills, for exactly the same reason that many organizations offer senior citizens driving skill refresher classes hoping to improve highway safety.

When I interviewed armed self-defense instructor Tom Givens, he made this comparison so well that I would like to quote his exact words—

Shooting is a perishable skill, Givens explains, and he compares continued training to something nearly every American does, driving a car. "Even though they drive a car every day, most people don't drive a car terribly well, because they weren't trained correctly and they don't get sustainment training on it, but they get by with it because they drive a car on a daily basis," he compares. "Very few people shoot on a daily basis."

"To use that car analogy, let's say that you don't know how to drive a car. Somebody spends eight hours–and that's all, eight hours–teaching you how to drive a car, and then you never drive that car again for months or years, but you've got the keys hanging there on the wall by the door. The theory is that if there is a sudden, life-threatening crisis that only you can fix, grab those keys, jump in the

This replica Colt Single-Action Army revolver has a notch in the hammer that serves as the rear sight, and nothing more.

This S&W Model 686 revolver's front and rear sights are larger.

LEFT: *Traditional sight alignment shown on Glock auto pistol.*

RIGHT: *Traditional sight alignment shown on Smith & Wesson Model 60 revolver.*

LEFT: *Shooting "out of the notch," the competitors' term for StressPoint Index, shows the view seen by the shooter using this speed technique.*

ABOVE: *Cirillo's Weapon Silhouette for the semi-automatic calls for viewing the gun squarely from behind, so you do not see the flat sides of the slide. This is a quick way to ascertain that the gun is pointed straight at the target, not off to one side.*

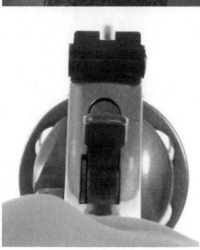

LEFT: *Weapon Silhouette for the revolver as defined by Jim Cirillo, gives the shooter a view of an entirely round cylinder.*

car and drive off at 100 miles an hour. Somebody who didn't know how to drive, only had eight hours of driving training, and hasn't driven in the last two or three years, is going to have a really hard time doing that."

"It is the same with a gun. You take eight hours of training with a pistol, you learn the basic manipulations, and then you don't handle the gun, you don't shoot, you don't practice, you don't get your sustainment training, and two or three years down the pike you need that gun RIGHT NOW! In the next couple of seconds, you are either going to live or die. If you really expect to pull that off, I'd suggest that you might be a little optimistic."

"So that's exactly where we are at with the handgun. We've got to get initial training so we can do things correctly, and then have sustainment training so we continue to do things correctly." [3]

I've never heard it said better, and if you have the chance to take a class with Tom and his wife Lynn, either at their Memphis, TN, facility, Rangemaster, TN, or when they travel as guest instructors at ranges around the country, do not miss the chance to learn from them.

Without practiced skills, the mere possession of any tool is of little benefit. The value of the self-defense handgun is strictly in proportion to the skill and skill-borne confidence of its user. Let's keep that in mind as we go on to discuss learning how to use handguns for concealed carry.

ABOVE & LEFT: *Crimson Trace's laser sighting products include the Laser Grip and LaserGuard products.*

(1) Safe Direction Ballistic Containment Products from Ravelin Group, LLC, 426 S. Westgate, Suite S-1, Addison, IL 60101, 630-834-4423, http://www.ravelingroup.com/safedirection.html

(2) Kathy Jackson's Cornered Cat Training Company, P.O. Box 396, Onalaska, WA 98570 www.cornered cat.com, pax@corneredcat.com

(3) Tom Givens, quoted in August 2012 journal of the Armed Citizens' Legal Defense Network, Inc. http://www.armedcitizensnetwork.org/our-journal/271-july-2012?start=6

CONCEALED CARRY SKILLS

Let's share some ideas about learning and practicing safe draw and fire, picking up speed, drawing from concealment and more…all the while focusing on safety, safety, safety!

How can you decide what shooting skills you might need to defend yourself? Study assault reports, put yourself in the victim's shoes and ask how the dangerous situation could have been better resolved. How far apart were the participants? Was it light, dark, extremely crowded or isolated? What other problems were present? That might include partial or moving targets, intervening obstacles, or the presence of other innocents who must not be hit. Realistically preparing to use a handgun for self defense out in public requires higher skill levels than being able to shoot a nice six-inch shot group on a sunny day from the 15 yard line, on a static shooting range where targets do not move and you do not have to move, either. Realistic defensive shooting skills must take into consideration multiple distractions, emotions, verbal interaction with assailants, moving and shooting, targets that move, adverse lighting and other unfavorable environmental conditions. In short, it calls for strong intermediate to advanced level skills. Build your shooting abilities until you qualify to participate in force-on-force training, where you can practice a spectrum of defensive strategies under realistic simulations.

Society requires that police officers complete about 80 hours of firearms training plus participate in regular in-service updates, a standard that may or may not be sufficient, but at least it establishes some minimum expectations. This is the standard set for armed professionals who will carry a gun into dangerous situations. How different is the armed citizen's defensive gun use? Distilled to its essence—using a gun to stop or subdue an assailant—the fundamental skills are the same. The differences are found in the frequency of exposure to danger and the officer's duty to control an offender, where an armed citizen can and should try to make their escape whenever possible. That is the greatest difference. When the gun is drawn and shooting is the only way out, the skills that assure accurate hits are identical. Don't be satisfied with your level of training after you have completed the eight- or twelve-hour licensing class your state probably requires prior to issuing a license to carry a concealed handgun. Don't stop studying after completing a challenging two-day defensive handgun class. Keep training and keep learning. Make skill maintenance and taking on growth challenges a lifetime habit.

What kind of gun skills may be required for self defense? Our active imaginations conjure scenarios that resemble a horror movie in which a man in the shadows brandishes a long, sharp knife as we hurry down an empty alley. Movies leave us expecting several minutes warning of impending danger, mounting anxiety, growing to a crescendo of horror that eventually explodes in an attack. In reality, assaults are either unpredictable ambushes or they occur in situations in which we find we cannot control an aggressor who we

Preparing to use a handgun for self defense requires higher skill levels than being able to shoot a nice six-inch shot group on a sunny day.

may often know, as when women fall victim to workplace violence, date rape or domestic violence, to name only a few examples. In both situations, as in nearly every other defensive gun use, the attack is overwhelming and explosive and the aggressor employs violence to shock the intended victim into submission.

The very short timelines common in ambush attacks are of considerable concern for the concealed carry practitioner. Obviously, a gun carried concealed needs to be hidden from view, but at the same time, it needs to be immediately available. When a student asked how long he would have to draw a gun and shoot, armed self defense instructor John Farnam [1] is said to have coined this axiom, "You will have the rest of your life." With time at such a premium, you do not have the luxury of stopping to think about what to do next. You have time to react based on experience, training and prior mental preparation.

HOLSTER WORK

Drawing the gun from its holster is one of the skills we train and practice so that the steps involved in bringing the gun out from beneath concealing clothing and up on target come automatically when they are needed. This is most effective if the personal defense handgun is carried in the same location and in the same manner consistently. While the preliminary steps of drawing a gun are somewhat influenced by the type of clothing covering the gun, with creativity, the concealed carry practitioner can enjoy wearing a variety of fashions while carrying the gun in the same location so the repetitions from practice can pay off when drawing quickly is required.

People conceal guns in a plethora of body locations, as will be illustrated in future chapters outlining the considerable variety of holsters commercially available. If you are just getting started with concealed carry, I strongly advise

you to start by learning to use a standard belt holster, though you can adjust where you position your gun on your waistline to attain the best balance of concealability and comfort for your individual shape.

Why should beginners start with a belt holster? First, in this holster type you will find the greatest number of commercially available holsters from which to choose, and the greatest likelihood that a reasonable number of safe holsters will be made for the model of gun you carry.

Next, most firearms trainers prefer to teach live fire exercises working from a belt holster, so by carrying your handgun in a similar way you can maximize the benefits of your training expenses. A belt holster also provides

Drawing from a belt holster accomplished by first flipping a concealment vest out of the way to grab the grips of the revolver carried in this Mitch Rosen Nancy Special belt holster.

the safest platform from which to draw and to holster a loaded firearm in a multi-student class environment. The beginner needs the ability to take full advantage of training opportunities, while enjoying a good number of holster options from which to choose. Obtaining and learning to use a belt holster provides both. As your skill, experience and training expands, you can branch out to additional carry methods if you find that you need them.

Before dealing with drawing from beneath clothing that conceals a handgun, we need to make sure we know how to safely draw from a belt holster. Later, we will discuss in the same detail drawing from alternative carry modes, but for now we need to learn the basics so we have a good foundation upon which to build.

The tactical ready position puts the shooter's hands in ready position from which she can draw quickly, but the posture does not look strained or aggressive until the armed citizen reaches for the holstered gun. This position lets us stand in the line at the bank or pizza parlor, with hands ready to access a belt holstered gun, without attracting unwanted attention.

Get a good firing grip on the gun while it is still in the holster. Pay special attention to the trigger finger position as shooter prepares to draw. The finger will not go on the trigger until the pistol's sights are on target.

Concealed carry practitioners who carry in a belt holster learn to stand with their gun-side hip angled slightly away from other people, and generally hands should be held naturally around the mid-line of the body. Not only does this leave hands ready to block an incoming blow or grab, it positions the strong side arm or elbow where it can inconspicuously cover the holstered gun if you are in a crowded area where someone may bump into and discover your gun or if you fear the gun may be grabbed and taken away from you by an aggressor.

When the handgun is in a belt holster, it remains readily at hand in a consistent position and it is stable so you can quickly get a good grip that accommodates fast and accurate shooting. Nowhere in the steps between drawing the handgun and firing the shot is attaining a proper shooting grip so easily achieved as when the gun is secured in the holster. Thus, the first step in drawing from a holster is to position the hand as high on the grips of the gun as possible, with the middle, ring and pinky fingers closed firmly around the grips

This high-quality holster designed by shooter Cerisse Wilson of Soteria Leather [2] will accommodate a full shooting grip while the gun is still in holster. It leaves plenty of room for the middle finger to close in a fist around the grips of the gun without any impediment from the mouth of the holster.

of the gun. The trigger finger is extended straight and somewhat away from the gun. The rest of the grip looks like a one handed version of the position of your hands as you fire your handgun.

The quality of a holster's design can be judged by how well a holster accommodates getting the shooting grip while the gun is still in the holster. Good holster design should allow the shooting hand's thumb to slip between the gun and body, completing the closed fist on the grips of the gun. If the holster gets in the way of either the thumb or your middle finger as you attempt to close a full fist around the grips of the gun, it may need minor modifications or simply is not designed well and you may need to replace it with something better.

Believe it or not, the commercial aspect of the firearm industry includes a number of designers, engineers and craftsmen who, while experts at what they do and know, do not have training and experience as shooters and do not carry guns. While there exist exceptionally experienced shooters-turned-inventors who do make concealed carry gear, don't be surprised when you learn that a certain amount of what is marketed for concealed carry is really not functional. With holsters, this is often revealed when the shooter attempts to get a shooting grip on the gun in the holster. If the holster interferes with proper technique, replace it.

Once you have a strong shooting grip on the holstered gun, draw it up and out straight along the axis of the holster. In other words, if the holster sits absolutely vertical on your belt (straight up and down), draw the gun straight up and out of the holster. If the holster has a forward or rearward cant, draw the gun out following the angle of the holster. If you twist the gun before it is clear of the holster, the front sight may snag inside, or the entire gun will bind in the holster and the holster will attempt to follow the gun up. While we laugh with students who suffer wedgies when gun, holster, belt and trousers follow the drawing hand up while they are on the training range, this problem slows the draw, and if you have "the rest of your life" to get the gun out, you'll really wish you'd worked out the draw before your life depended on it.

With a gun carried in a strong side belt holster, when the muzzle of the gun is clear of the top of the holster, the elbow of the drawing arm is probably approaching shoulder-level. Keeping your wrist locked and straight, simply drop that elbow to your ribcage, orienting the gun toward the target at about waist height. At the same time, bring the gun hand to your mid-line where the support hand is waiting from the tactical ready position described earlier. Keep the support hand close to your body until the gun's muzzle is forward of it, then feed the gun hand into the fingers of the support hand and form a solid two handed grip.

Strong side belt carry does impose an extreme lift of the elbow to draw the gun as the photos show. The shorter-waisted women find this quite a contortion, especially when wearing trousers at the natural waistline, so may prefer fashions with waistbands sitting at hip level, below the natural waistline. Alternatively, the steps to draw (called the draw stroke) for a belt holstered handgun positioned forward of the hip, in what is called appendix carry or carried cross draw, do not entail the same contortions.

When the gun and holster are carried forward of the hip, a number of additional safety concerns, which we'll cover later, come into play, but the

Sometimes a dropped and offset holster may follow the gun during the draw stroke. Drawing the gun at a bit of an angle is usually to blame, and the longer the offset shank, the more exaggerated this error seems.

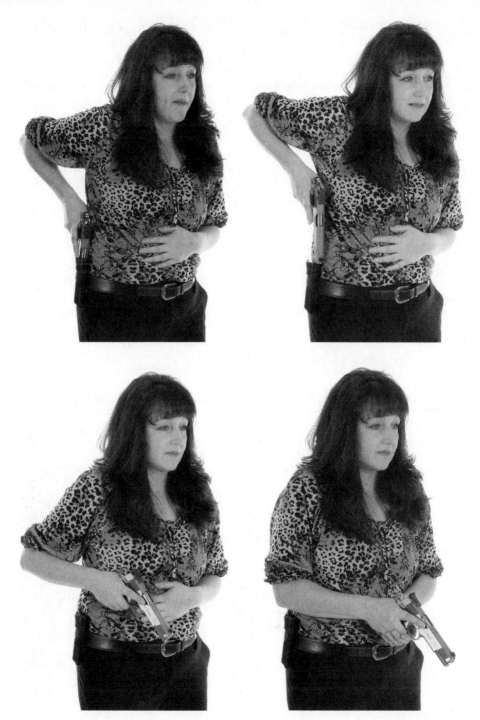

Melissa demonstrates the draw and presentation stroke from a holster positioned behind the strong side hip. The holster sits a little high, so you will notice the considerable elbow lift necessary for her to draw the long-barreled gun out of this particular holster.

In preparing to draw, the hands start at the tactical ready position, then separate as the non-dominant hand moves to a safe location away from the muzzle's path and the dominant hand blurs as it races to the grips of the gun.

Draw and presentation stroke for the cross draw carry is similar to appendix carry, starting with a vigorous upward tug on the sweater to lift it out of the way, then exercising care to get the gun far enough ahead of the body before dropping the off hand behind the gun so it is never in front of the muzzle.

Kathy's draw and presentation stroke from the appendix carry position begins with hands aggressively forward, grabbing the hem of the covering garment and ripping it up so she can grip the gun, lift it from its holster, orient it toward the target and join her non-dominant hand in the two-handed grip while thrusting it toward target, ending in a strong Isosceles shooting position.

Though shooters carry their handgun in a variety of positions, our goal through training and practice is to learn a safe and fast technique to bring the gun from the holster to the fully extended position from which we can see the sights overlain on the target.

LEFT: *This holster sits a little too high. Despite Melissa's hip level waistband, by the time she gets the muzzle out of the holster, she had had to lift her elbow nearly above her shoulder and she strains to make the gear work for her. Can you imagine the struggle she would face if wearing slacks with a higher waistband?*

BELOW: *This holster sits a little too high for Diane's short-waisted figure. Despite the speed cut in this Rusty Sherrick high rise holster, by the time Diane gets the muzzle out of the holster, she had had to lift her elbow nearly above her shoulder.*

Help comes with every inch the holster sits lower! Diane's elbow lift is alleviated somewhat by using a Blade Tech holster that sits a little lower on the belt and incorporates a speed cut so the muzzle comes out of the holster with less vertical lift.

draw stroke is a simple lift up and out of the holster, after which the shooter orients the muzzle toward the target. It is little wonder that many women prefer to carry their handguns forward of the hip.

After the gun has been drawn, and with both hands closed firmly around the grip, thrust it forward into the ready position or the firing position as dictated the circumstances. Appropriate aiming technique and trigger control will yield good hits on target, because this efficient drawing sequence assures that you start with a good shooting grip on the handgun and that the gun comes up roughly aligned on target.

Consistency in shooting hand and support hand position on the handgun's grips is extremely important, because without achieving a uniform hand position every time you draw, the trigger finger may not be in position to apply strong, straight-back pressure on the trigger, and the resulting struggle to complete the trigger pull moves the muzzle of the gun off to one side or another, away from the center of the target. These problems are avoided by getting a good shooting grip that starts when the shooting hand grasps the holstered gun. This is why a good belt holster is so very important.

Defensive shooting skills are extremely holistic in nature. All of the elements of how the gun is carried and how it is drawn and presented to target must support

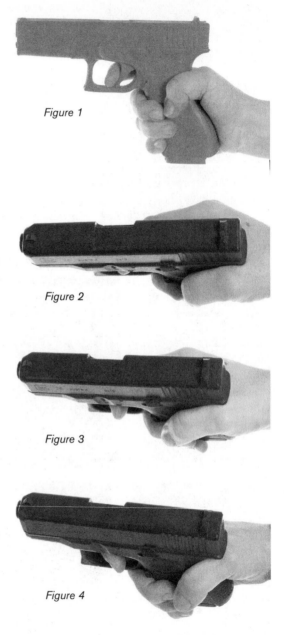

Figure 1

Figure 2

Figure 3

Figure 4

Grip errors: Fig. 1 - Too low; Fig. 2 - Not enough finger reaching the trigger; Fig. 3 - Optimum grip with crease of trigger finger contacting center face of the trigger; Fig. 4 - Too much of the trigger finger wrapped over the trigger, with thumb knuckle in contact with backstrap where it will take a beating.

aiming and must put the shooter in the position to exercise good trigger control. If the holster is poorly designed and you are unable to get a good shooting grip in the holster, a good end result is impossible to achieve at realistic defensive speeds where every element must be working at maximum efficiency.

Both hands will not always be available when you need to draw and shoot in self defense, so realistic training should address one-handed shooting. You need to be able to draw one-handed, since your support hand, while helpful to stabilize the handgun, may instead be necessarily occupied guiding a child or other dependent person out of harm's way or may be holding a phone on which you have dialed 9-1-1 in the moment before a lesser threat escalated into a deadly one.

You may find it curious to learn that safely returning the gun to the holster can be nearly as critical as drawing it out. Few self-defense incidents occur in a vacuum. If you are fortunate, law enforcement officers should be on their way to help you not long after you drew your gun, and you need a plan to get the gun out of your hands before police arrive on the scene and mistake you for the assailant. Understand that most police calls involving people with guns also involve the commission of a violent crime, so the subliminal association of a gun with a violent criminal is nearly unavoidable. You need to be able to get the gun out of your hands a moment before police arrive to take over the scene.

Ready, easy accessibility that makes it easy to insert the drawn gun back into the holster is essential, especially when you must keep your eyes on an attacker who seconds ago was trying to take your life, while also interacting with other participants on the scene, as well as identifying yourself for police officers when they approach. This is no time to be fumbling with a holster that has collapsed flat and closed up as soon as the gun came out, or looking down to locate a holster that has slipped to a different position, or inferior equipment that otherwise blocks the safe holstering of the gun.

You also need to be prepared for less well-defined circumstances in which you may have drawn the gun only to find, thankfully, that shooting it is not necessary. In addition, armed citizens and trainers rarely acknowledge it, but occasionally the armed defender misreads a threatening situation or reacts precipitously and brings out a gun when use of deadly force is not yet warranted. While the risky situation may still need defusing, getting the gun quickly out of sight and out of your hands may make a big difference. It is a bad idea to be standing around in public with a drawn gun, especially if you misread a situation and drew when you were not justified in using deadly force.

In a situation for which you believe use of deadly force is the only solution, your body will have pumped adrenaline and other hormones into your bloodstream the after effects of which include tremors, loss of manual dexterity and loss of sensation in the extremities. All these side effects make decocking the gun, engaging its safety, and safely putting it back into its holster challenging indeed. Concealed carry methods for which holstering when the holster is only marginally safe are disasters waiting to happen when the armed citizen is shaky and distracted, gasping for breath and needing to put the gun away quickly. Do not believe the hacks who tell you that holstering after a fight is a non-issue and doesn't really matter. It does.

Finally, to our great, good fortune, armed citizens rarely draw and present a gun in self defense. The serious self defense practitioner will, however, draw, present, fire and return her handgun to the holster millions of times in training and practice. When draw, fire and holstering skills are practiced with live ammunition, the safety with which the gun can be holstered is extremely important.

Too often, student shooters feel they must pry the holster open with the fingers of their non-dominant hand before they can slip the muzzle into the mouth of the holster. Trainers often jump in to stop the student's the non-gun hand from coming back to the mouth of the holster even with well-made holsters that remain open. I can only hypothesize that the shooter is apparently driven by an urge to feel for the holster's location to guide the gun inside. Whatever the motivation,

Returning the gun safely to a hip holster with the muzzle pointing forward or away from the body until the muzzle has started into the mouth of the holster, at which point the gun is tipped down into holster, index finger pointing out away from trigger, then seated firmly and fully in the holster.

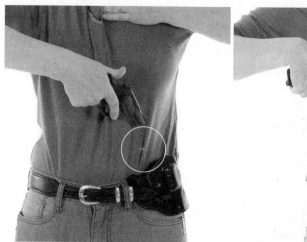

How NOT to do it—Laser dot shows that the muzzle has pointed into the body cavity where an unintentional discharge would cause devastating injury.

The same safe holstering steps shown for a holster in the appendix position, with Kathy showing how to exercise great care to lean backward to make sure the gun is not pointing at the femoral artery or into the body cavity, as well as pointing the finger far away from the trigger during holstering for added safety.

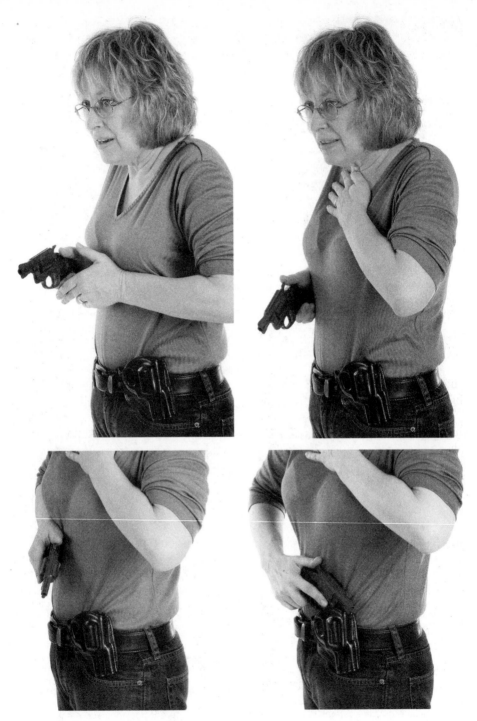

Safe holstering shown for cross draw carry includes getting the non-dominant hand well out of the path of the muzzle and making extra sure that the muzzle points away from the body at all times.

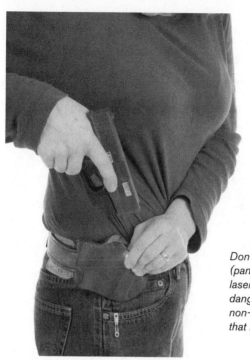

Don't do this! The problem with pancakes (pancake holsters, that is…) shown with a laser-equipped Ring's Blue Gun to highlight the danger to fingers when the shooter uses the non-dominant hand to pry open a soft holster that has closed up without the gun inside.

this is extremely dangerous, as it puts the non-dominant hand's fingers in front of the gun muzzle.

Other times, shooters angle the muzzle toward the body cavity when returning the gun to the holster. If it discharged, they would suffer an abdominal gunshot wound along with damage to pelvic or hipbone structure. Another variation of failing to control muzzle direction during holstering is the rearward stab made as the shooter tries to get the muzzle into the holster. If anyone were standing behind them, an accidental shot caused by a finger on the trigger, or clothing or a retention strap snagging in the trigger guard, would wound onlookers.

None of that is acceptable! If you observe it on the range while you are practicing or training, make a firmly worded request that it cease immediately, and if the muzzle control safety issues are not resolved, leave the range because apparently safety is not the management's first priority. If you are guilty of any of these safety violations, embark on a strict dryfire training regimen until you have learned how to safely draw and return your gun to the holster. Do not work with a loaded gun until you can undertake the draw and holster steps in complete safety.

Since we see, and thus better control the area forward of our bodies, it is best to return the gun to the holster with the muzzle pointing forward until the gun is safely inside the holster. This takes practice and some physical flexibility. Bring the gun down out of the firing position keeping the muzzle pointing forward, still in your firing grip, with your index finger far outside the trigger guard and high up on the frame.

If you need to look at your holster to remind your hand where to go, by all means, look during early practice to learn the skill! With enough practice, look-

The teaching coach standing behind a shooter holstering a Blue Gun equipped with a laser shows how injury can occur if the shooter does not bring the gun to the mouth of the holster with the muzzle pointing forward and downrange. Since accidents happen more frequently during holstering than any other gun handling chore, it is essential that shooters learn to point the muzzle forward until it starts into the holster.

Kathy demonstrates the 360-degree danger scan before she holsters.

ing will become unnecessary, but until you attain that level of proficiency, it is not acceptable to stab the muzzle around until miraculously you find the mouth of the holster. It is all right to be a learner, it is all right to be a novice, as long as we are improving our skills and working to gain proficiency. Unsafe gun handling procedures in an attempt to appear more accomplished than we really are absolutely are not acceptable.

As the muzzle of the gun is slipped into the mouth of the holster, rotate the gun from its muzzle-forward orientation to match the angle of the holster and slip the gun fully inside the holster. Maintain your grip, though holding the trigger finger away from the gun and holster, and pause for a moment or two as you seat the gun in the holster and look around your environment in a 360-degree safety scan. We habituate this safety procedure during practice and training so that in a real emergency the return of the gun to the holster does not psychologically signal the "all clear" to return to complete safety in an environment that has only moments earlier proven dangerous. Remain on guard and scan for additional dangers.

A well-made holster supports realistic practice and safe training. If the holster or carry method you currently employ cannot support drawing or reholstering safely without pointing the gun at yourself or another person, get rid of it and buy a safer carry system. Don't settle for anything less.

---

(1) Soteria Leather, http://www.soterialeather.com 360-952-1535

(2) John Farnam, Defense Training International, P.O. Box 917, LaPorte, CO 80535, 970-482-2520, http://www.defense-training.com

INTRODUCTION TO HANDGUNS FOR CONCEALED CARRY

Let's discuss choosing a gun for concealed carry. When choosing one from literally hundreds, if not thousands, of handgun models available, it helps to establish some guidelines so you can eliminate what is not appropriate for your needs. Making a list of priorities helps reduce the options to a manageable number from which you can make a smart choice.

Never have armed citizens enjoyed such a variety of handguns for concealed carry! In the 1960s and 1970s when the practice of concealed carry was getting a foothold, the armed citizen bought a snub-nosed revolver, or maybe a .32 or .380 Walther PPK. Today, overwhelming numbers make it hard to count all the guns designed especially for the concealed carry market. Specific models and manufacturers are too numerous to list here. Instead, we'll explain the differences between revolvers, semi-automatics, double-action or single-action semi-autos, and even derringers and other less mainstream options, and outline the pros and cons for each. Some of these guns make good concealed carry choices and some are not so good.

Deciding between a particular style of gun and the caliber of ammunition it will fire is something of a chicken and egg question. Which comes first and how should you decide what handgun in which caliber you wish to carry?

First, let's make sure we establish the vocabulary necessary for this conversation.

CALIBER

First, what does "caliber" mean? Technically, caliber identifies the diameter of the inside of the gun barrel or bore, and the diameter of the bullet of the ammunition that will be fired through that barrel. This definition is broadly applied to ammunition and for example the bullet in a .45 ACP cartridge of ammunition measures approximately .45-inch across its widest point. In addition to being stated as fractions of inches, handgun caliber may be expressed in millimeters, as is done for the common 9mm.

The actual numeric citation is nominal in some cases, because many handgun calibers are so old that their dimensions have evolved slightly. Shooters, being a tradition-loving folk, are loath to abandon a caliber's name and history. Thus, a .38 Special handgun fires a bullet with an actual diameter .355 of an inch inside a case diameter of .357-.358 of an inch, obviously a far cry from 38/100th of an inch described by the name.

When speaking of a gun's caliber, we further identify a cartridge's overall length, general shape or profile, and the pressures built up inside the case before the bullet is propelled down the barrel, since it would be wildly inaccurate to believe that all cartridges using a projectile measuring 45/100ths of an inch are the same or even similar!

Since the term caliber identifies further distinctions beyond the bore and bullet diameter, caliber will usually include an additional set of initials. This fact is important to your overall understanding of handgun caliber, because, for example, when you buy guns and ammunition, you will find .380 ACP, .38 Special, and .38 Super ammunition, which you would probably guess by their second names, "ACP," "Special" and "Super," are somehow different despite sharing a common diameter. Your guess would be right. Overall length is different, and in addition, the .38 Special cartridge uses a rimmed case that is radically different

The muzzle of a Kahr Arms 9mm semi-automatic pistol shown with the components comprising a 9mm cartridge of centerfire ammunition, including a primer, powder, case and bullet.

Using the .38 caliber as just one common cause of caliber confusion, we see the .380 ACP cartridge for semi-auto atop a box and samples of .38 Special cartridges, which are customarily fired through a revolver. Other potential mistakes with .38s include the .38 Super, since the numeric element in this semi-automatic cartridge's name provides yet another possibility for mistaken cartridge identity.

from the rimless cases of the .380 ACP and .38 Super. Each is of a different length and the case pressures when the ammunition is fired are quite unalike, as well. These are some of the critical factors preventing safe or successful cross-use of these similar yet very different calibers. Still, some potential for error exists, and for safety's sake you must exercise caution to fire only ammunition of the correct caliber for your handgun!

If uncertain about these details, find a good instructor with whom to study or confirm what you have been taught through reference books like John Farnam's *The Farnam Method of Defensive Handgunning*[1] or the guns and ammunition chapters in my earlier book *Personal Defense for Women* by this book's publisher.[2]

By now, you may have guessed that there are hundreds of various calibers of ammunition made for the nearly endless variety of firearms. Of handguns alone, I can think of at least thirty handgun calibers that are in current production, and many more which have faded away to take their place in the annals of handgunning.

Other unusual calibers are extremely specialized, though, to the extent that you would not be able to walk into a sizeable gun store, even one of the large outdoor and shooting chain stores, and always find both a handgun and ammunition readily available in that caliber.

Limited availability is a clue to which you want to pay attention! If you choose a mainstream handgun caliber, it is much easier to find guns, ammunition and related accessories like holsters or parts like spare magazines or aftermarket sights in the gun stores. Having the "only gun like this in a five-state region" might be fun if you are a collector, but it is not a smart idea at all for the handgun you choose for daily defense. Rare caliber handguns are a serious disadvantage when ammunition is not readily available in gun stores, is available only by special order or, because the caliber is unusual, retails for a premium price. Considering today's already high ammunition prices, supporting a handgun that

Common handgun ammunition (left to right), 10mm, .45 ACP, .40 S&W, 9x19 aka 9mm Parabellum, 9x18 aka 9mm Makarov, .380 ACP aka 9x17, .32 ACP and .22 LR.

Rimmed and rimless cartridges, illustrated by .45 ACP (left), which is rimless, and .38 Special (right), with a rimmed case.

requires expensive, special ammunition is a chilling prospect, indeed.

Though the subject of handgun and ammunition caliber is one of considerable depth (and it is covered in greater detail in my earlier book *Personal Defense for Women*), you will be in a solid position if you choose a handgun chambered for centerfire cartridges in calibers .380 ACP, .38 Special, .357 Magnum, 9mm, .40 S&W, or .45 ACP. These are the most common calibers in a good range of self-defense choices, though there are certainly many less prominent calibers in this power range. Additionally, there exist both smaller and larger calibers, though they tend to be either not sufficiently powerful or excessively powerful for the self-defense mission, as would be the situation with either a .17 HMR varmint handgun or a .44 Magnum hunting handgun, for example. Just like the chairs in the Goldilocks fairytale, the first is too small and the other is too big! Finally, there also exist a number of specialized calibers like the .32 NAA, .327 Magnum, .357 Sig and .45 GAP, 10mm, .44 Special, .41 Magnum, .45 Colt, .50 AE to name only a few, but the availability and cost of ammunition will severely inhibit how much you can shoot and thus polish your self-defense skills.

Cartridges in .380 ACP, .38 Special, .357 Magnum, 9mm, .40 S&W, or .45 ACP are further divided by the guns in which they are designed to fire, with rimmed cartridges like the .38 Special and .357 Magnum commonly fired in revolvers, and rimless cartridges generally fired through semi-automatic pistols. Of course, there are exceptions to both generalizations, and we also have to fac-

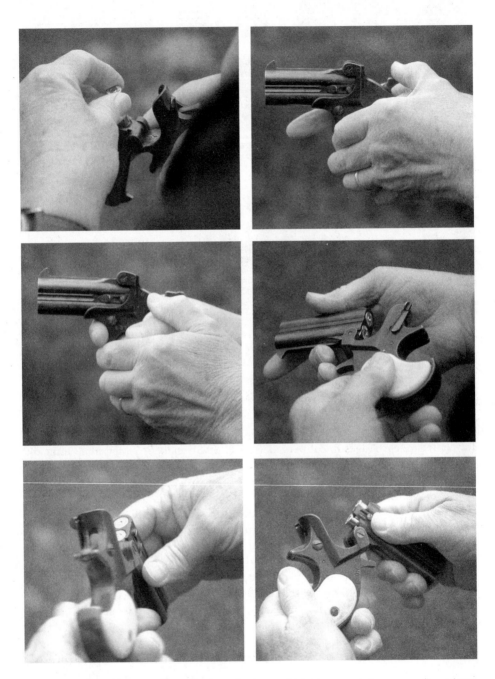

Loading, shooting and unloading a derringer is slow and laborious, even for an experienced gun aficionado like Clay Whitehead. With only two rounds of ammunition available, a derringer is insufficient for self defense.

This is the difference between single- and double-action revolvers: Replica of a Colt Single-Action Army revolver (front) has to be manually cocked by the shooter's thumb. The Smith & Wesson Model 686 double-action revolver (back) operates by trigger cocking. As the shooter pulls the double-action trigger of the 686, the hammer is simultaneously cocked by the same action. With both operating systems, as the shooter reaches the end of the trigger pull, the hammer is released to fall forward and discharge the cartridge of ammunition.

Loading, shooting and unloading a Single-Action Army revolver replica.

tor in semi-rimmed cartridges. Finding a good gun for personal protection and concealed carry doesn't rely on fully understanding all the technicalities, though if you find it interesting, as do I, you might enjoy browsing through some of the traditional gun collector books.

HANDGUN TYPES

Handguns suitable for personal defense can be divided into two action types: double-action revolvers and semi-automatic handguns. While they are fun to shoot, single-action revolvers and derringers aren't suitable for defense work. Single-action revolvers require a separate motion to manually cock the hammer for

RIGHT: *Cartridges are loaded into the chambers of the cylinder of the double-action revolver, shown here, one with the action open, the other closed.*

LEFT: *Two Glock semi-autos, one (left) shown with the magazine seated and action closed, a condition sometimes called "in battery," from which it could be fired if loaded and one (right) with the action open and magazine out.*

each shot and are slow to unload and reload since the loading gate allows access to only one chamber in the cylinder at a time. Derringers also have to be manually cocked before the can be discharged, and they only contain two cartridges of ammunition. As such, they do not have the ammunition capacity for reliable self defense, since they're insufficient when stopping a determined assailant requiring a number of shots, to say nothing of the common problem of multiple assailants.

That narrows the gun selection field to either a double-action revolver or a semi-automatic pistol for concealed carry for personal defense. Both are fine choices and neither is necessarily better than the other. Choosing between a double-action revolver and a semi-automatic pistol is a very individual decision. The choice depends on what fits your needs and what you prefer. If you are new to guns and you are not sure which type to pick, find an introductory handgun class that provides guns for the students to use and make an educated decision that is based on your own experience before you buy a gun. In addition, a lot of indoor gun ranges have gun rental counters, and once you have attended training and learned gun safety and the fundamentals of handgun operation, rental guns at indoor ranges provide a great opportunity to try out specific gun models before making a purchase.

Loading the double-action revolver using a speed loader: Grasping the barrel of the speedloader instead of the tiny release knob, shooter feeds tips of the bullets into the chambers and seats the speed loader. After giving the release handle a twist, the speedloader is released to fall to the ground, where it can be collected later when the pressure to get the gun back into action has abated.

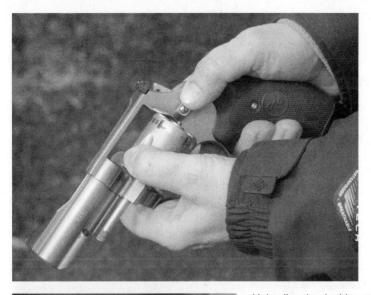

Unloading the double-action revolver starts by bringing it down out of the firing plane, moving the dominant thumb to the cylinder release and pressing as the support hand moves to grasp the cylinder and push it out. The revolver is then inverted, and the heel of the dominant hand strikes the ejector rod, kicking the empty cartridge cases out of the chambers.

THE READY REVOLVER

Many shooters prefer the double-action revolver for self defense carry because its operation is mechanically quite simple. It arguably has fewer moving parts about which one must be concerned when evaluating both durability and reliability, as well as weighing the potential for operator error. The double-action revolver consists of a grip, frame, barrel and a cylinder that locks into the frame until the shooter opens the action and tips the cylinder out for either loading or unloading. The cylinder must be locked in the frame for the revolver to fire, which we describe as having the action closed.

Some revolvers are modified to load with moon clips so rimless cartridges like 9mm or .45 ACP ammunition can be fired. Loading and unloading moon clip equipped revolvers is very fast, so it is not unusual to see this modification in use at competitive shooting events.

Generally, revolvers do not have manual safeties. The shooter must put pressure on the trigger to both cock and release the hammer. That pressure ranges between 10 to 15 pounds of trigger pull weight distributed over about an inch of pull, and requires a conscious movement of the trigger finger to accomplish. This has caused some to celebrate the simplicity of shooting a revolver–just point, aim and shoot, they say. That perceived advantage is mitigated somewhat by the steps required to reload a low-capacity revolver, though with practice and skill this task can be accomplished quite rapidly. In addition, hand strength is needed to succeed with a double-action revolver, as we see when students struggle to complete the trigger pull, especially time and time again as is required at a training class.

Like most guns, revolvers come in a variety of calibers. For defensive purposes, it's best to stick with .38 Special or .357 Magnum. Alternatives include the more specialized .327 Federal Magnum, or revolvers modified to fire 9mm, .40 or .45 caliber cartridges; the first is disadvantaged by being somewhat unusual and may suffer ammunition supply problems, and the latter three generally require a special metal clip to position the cartridges properly in the cylinder. Moon clips are usually a special order item you won't find on gun store shelves, and the thin metal cartridge holders can be bent if stepped on or otherwise abused.

There certainly are larger caliber revolvers: .44 Special, .41 Magnum, .44 Magnum, 454 Casull, .50 S&W come quickly to mind, but for the purposes of a gun well-suited to concealed carry, those are too large and too recoil intensive. Likewise, there are certainly plenty of smaller caliber revolvers, chambered in .17 Hornady, a variety of .22 calibers, .32 H&R and others, but for self defense, we should stick with calibers recognized for having more reliable stopping power.

THE SOPHISTICATED SEMI-AUTOMATIC

Pressing the revolver's trigger both lines up the cartridge and cocks and releases the hammer to strike the firing pin and discharge the gun. When pressing the trigger of a semi-automatic handgun, part of the power of the discharging cartridge is harnessed to prepare for the next shot by cocking the hammer and moving a fresh cartridge into the firing chamber after removing the empty case from the previous shot.

The semi-automatic pistol is a magazine-fed gun, with ammunition loaded in a box magazine that in most designs is inserted into the hollow grips of the gun. From the top of the magazine, a cartridge of ammunition will be swept forward into the firing chamber when the shooter racks the gun's slide and releases it to

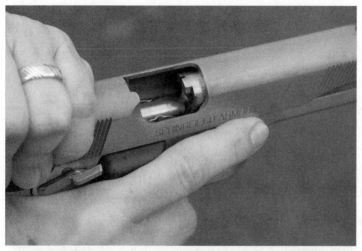

After putting the magazine in the gun, the shooter racks the slide, feeding a cartridge of ammunition off the top of the magazine, up the feed ramp and into the chamber. Skilled photographer using a motordrive captures a semi-automatic 1911-style handgun's cycling sequence.

Camera records the sequence used to reload the semi-automatic pistol at speed. A magazine is inserted and firmly seated with an upward thrust of the non-dominant palm.

The hand then swivels up to grasp the slide, pulling it as far back as it will go, then releasing it crisply, so the slide can pick up a cartridge of ammunition off the top of the magazine and move it into the chamber as it slams forward under spring pressure. At the end of this sequence, the action is closed and the gun is ready to fire again.

When the gun fires, the pressures from the discharging cartridge slam the slide back, ejecting the empty case and feeding a new cartridge of ammunition into the chamber, where, if the shooter pulls the trigger again, it will discharge in the same operating cycle.

slam forward. Thus, to start the firing cycle, the shooter must manually load the chamber. Thereafter, some of the pressure from the fired cartridge pushes the slide back so that the extractor and ejector can remove the empty case. A large spring called the recoil spring immediately returns the slide forward and, if there is ammunition in the magazine, the slide's forward movement concurrently sweeps a fresh cartridge off the top of the magazine and into the chamber.

The semi-automatic pistols we use for self defense will repeat this cycle once for each time the trigger is pulled until the ammunition in the magazine is expended. The uninitiated sometimes mistake semi-automatic function for fully automatic. A fully automatic firearm will continue firing as long as the trigger is pressed and ammunition is available, so with fully automatic firearms multiple shots are fired with only one press of the trigger. This is not the case with the more common semi-automatic handgun which fires one shot only with each press of the trigger. Fully automatic weapons are primarily used by police and military and are not commonly used for concealed carry for personal protection.

Semi-automatic handguns are made in a dizzying variety of shapes, sizes and calibers, featuring quite a variety of operating levers and buttons and showing little uniformity from one brand or model to the next. The variations lose some of their ability to awe and confuse if we acknowledge that each pistol is nothing more than a handheld tool from which to discharge a cartridge of ammunition—essentially to launch a bullet from a highly pressurized chamber at an extreme rate of speed. Thus, a semi-automatic handgun will have a firing chamber and a barrel, a means of initiating the firing cycle which will be accomplished by either a firing pin or a striker, and a means of activating the firing pin or striker which will be either a hammer or internal cams that release a striker held under spring pressure. A mechanical step to replace the empty cartridge case with a fresh, unfired cartridge is required, and this is why the slide cycles backwards and returns forward, first ejecting the empty case and then refilling the chamber as long as there is ammunition in the magazine.

Other variations in semi-auto handgun design and function deal with holding in place and releasing the box magazine holding the ammunition, a lever to manually lock the gun's action open, a lever used to safely lower the hammer from cocked and single action to double action, a safety lever or button that must be disengaged to fire the gun, and a means to index where the bullet will hit, which requires, of course, the pistol sights. Perhaps manufacturers don't really want us to know just how simple a handgun is! In breaking down the limited number of functions included in firing a handgun, it becomes easier to decide what we need, like and want in a semi-automatic handgun for personal protection.

Although there are many calibers of semi-automatics sold, for self defense, calibers .380 ACP, 9mm Luger/Parabellum, .40 S&W and .45 ACP will prove the most readily available. There are, of course, calibers smaller than .380 that are really too small for self defense, plus runners up like the 9x17 Makarov, a variety of 9mm off shoots, .357 SIG, 10mm, .45 GAP, and several .50 calibers, but all of those are less common. requires, of course, the pistol sights. Perhaps manufacturers don't really want us to know just how simple a handgun is! In breaking down the limited number of functions included in firing a handgun, it becomes easier to decide

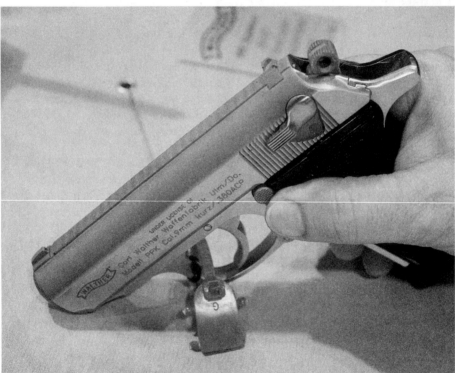

Magazine releases are located in various places on different brands and models of guns, including the most common position on the left side of the grips where the right hand thumb releases the magazine (UPPER), high up where the top corner of the grips meets the slide on this small Walther PPK (LOWER)...

...on the lower back of this Beretta Tomcat's grips...

...integrated into the trigger guard on this Walther P99 (LEFT) and at the base of the grips on this Ruger Mark II (BELOW).

Slide stops vary in shape and location from one brand and model of pistol to another, including this Glock auto pistol's thin, flat release on the left of the pistol frame (TOP), the rather complex one found on the third generation Smith & Wesson 3913 (RIGHT), no slide lock/ release whatsoever as is the case on this Walther PPK (BELOW).

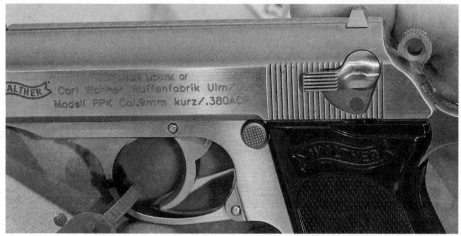

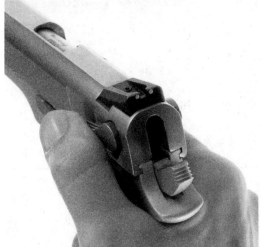

Decockers, to safely lower a cocked hammer, vary in shape and location from one brand and model of pistol to another, including Sig Sauer's decocking lever found forward of the grip on the left side (TOP), Smith & Wesson Model 3913's decocking lever (LEFT) doubles as the safety lever, as does the Walther PPK (BELOW) and many others.

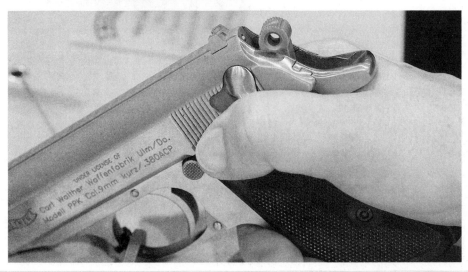

what we need, like and want in a semi-automatic handgun for personal protection.

Although there are many calibers of semi-automatics sold, for self defense, calibers .380 ACP, 9mm Luger/Parabellum, .40 S&W and .45 ACP will prove the most readily available. There are, of course, calibers smaller than .380 that are really too small for self defense, plus runners up like the 9x17 Makarov, a variety of 9mm off shoots, .357 SIG, 10mm, .45 GAP, and several .50 calibers, but all of those are less common.

Taurus' Model 92's decocking lever is designed to spring back to the "fire" position after safely lowering the hammer (UPPER), *and the Walther P99 has a decocker set flush in the top of the slide that the shooter depresses to safely place this unique striker fired pistol in double-action mode* (RIGHT).

SIZE AND WEIGHT

When shopping for a concealment gun, it is natural to gravitate to the tiniest pistols in the display shelves at the gun store. While I understand the buyers' thinking, that tendency creates several noteworthy problems. Why? As discussed in the introduction, the reason we carry guns is the possible need to shoot accurately and effectively to stop a violent criminal from harming our loved ones or us. This mission requires a reliable and user-friendly gun that can be employed with speed and accuracy, is equipped for ease of operation, and is chambered to fire an effective cartridge. That's a tall order, and many micro-pistols aren't up to the task.

The very small handguns are often chambered in small, ineffectual calibers that are too weak to reliably stop an assailant. They often sacrifice basic controls

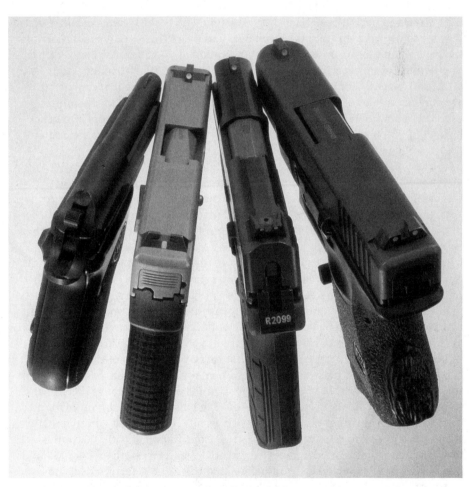

Choices, choices! (Right to left) Glock 26 is a better learner's gun than the smaller KelTec PF9 or Kahr PM9. The Beretta Model 21A is so small that it only chambers .22 LR ammunition, which is not sufficiently powerful for reliable self defense.

like a slide stop/slide release lever, lack large enough sights for accurate, aimed fire under pressure, and have such limited gripping surface that it is difficult to hold the tiny gun in a strong firing grip that is not disrupted while you pull the trigger. Further, if the grip is too small, the pistol recoils and can twist violently in the hand when fired because you simply cannot get a strong grip on so little gripping surface.

Like so many things, the size of your concealed carry handgun requires intelligent compromise. That compromise is between the size of handgun you can realistically conceal, weighed against making sure that you are carrying a handgun in an effective self-defense caliber that is adequately outfitted for the task of saving your life from a violent attacker.

WEIGHT IS A GOOD THING

Too many people mistakenly correlate gun weight with concealability. I have seen students make this mistake made over and over. This wrong conclusion fails the logic test because gun weight is no indication of overall dimension. In truth, overall dimension, especially the size of the grip, is the factor making a gun easy or hard to conceal, not its weight. As more and more guns are made using space-age polymer frames or extremely light metals like titanium or alloys combining titanium, aluminum or scandium, advertising has tricked consumers into believing a light gun is preferable for concealed carry. This is particularly apparent in the marketing of super lightweight alloy revolvers.

The worst problem with super lightweight guns is their punishing recoil, which only makes it that much harder to overcome the flinching reaction that plagues so many shooters. Firing .38 Special ammunition that merely creates a startling jump in a 20-ounce steel-framed revolver creates an abusive jolt of recoil in a 12-ounce alloy-framed gun. Too much of that and the shooter cannot help but anticipate the recoil and flinch away from it while firing the shot.

The 11-12-ounce super lightweight guns are intended for folks who want to carry their defense gun in a pocket. This carry method often isn't very practical for women since many of our clothes aren't made with large enough pockets to draw the gun out fast enough for emergency use. Besides, once you load the lightweight gun, adding a couple of more ounces of ammunition, the resulting 12 to 16 ounces is enough to make most clothing sag, unless wearing specially designed concealed carry garments. Why not carry a heavier steel-framed gun in a high-quality belt and holster and reap the benefits of a gun that is more comfortable to shoot? The weight of a concealment gun is not as critical as the size and ergonomics of the handgun you choose and the holster in which you carry it.

Still, when teaching classes, we see an awful lot of women whose first gun is an ultra-light alloy revolver, purchased without first firing 50-100 rounds through it or a similar model to determine how they react to the recoil. Many of these ladies have never fired a gun before, and their gun selection decisions rely on the opinions of others as they make their first gun purchase. Their advisors thinks, "This lady will just put her gun in her purse and never shoot it anyway." Others suggest, "She'll only shoot this gun a time or two, then put it in her

Aluminum framed S&W 642 (BOTTOM) weighs 15 ounces and appears identical in size to this all-steel S&W Model 640 (TOP) weighing 23 ounces, but the lighter aluminum-framed Model 642 will transmit more recoil to the shooter's hand. In addition, the larger Herrett's gun stocks on the all-steel version fills the hand and buffers recoil a bit better than the ultra-small boot grip Crimson Trace LaserGrip. The LaserGrip does bring the additional functionality of an aiming laser, offsetting the loss in comfort during firing.

purse." That insulting option may be a self-fulfilling prophecy, because firing full-power self-defense ammunition through a 12-ounce revolver is not an experience too many shooters will want to repeat over and over again!

Why are super light-weight guns so uncomfortable to shoot repeatedly? An 11-12-ounce gun simply does not have enough mass and weight to soak up the recoil created when firing the gun. The gun store clerk who sells a Taurus Model 85UL, a Charter Arms Lavender Lady or Smith & Wesson Model 340 scandium alloy revolver to a new female shooter for her primary gun while voicing the suggestion that "you'll never know it is in your purse" does a cruel disservice to a trusting customer. New shooters more than any others, need guns through which they can fire hundreds and thousands of rounds, as they train and practice to build up their skills. Failing to learn how to shoot the gun you carry is irresponsible. And finally, the "you'll never know this gun is even in your purse" sales pitch has never made any sense to me. Most purses are so full and heavy that an additional 12 to 16 ounces of a steel-framed revolver isn't going to make much difference! Besides, there are far safer ways to carry a gun than in a purse.

A handgun's usefulness in a self-defense emergency is only as great as its shooter's skills. As a shooter, your skills will increase in direct proportion to the time you spend training and practicing. A super lightweight gun makes effective training and practice very hard as it becomes increasingly difficult, if not impossible, to overcome the flinching reaction to recoil that all shooters must learn to manage. A gun that makes your hands sting and ache after firing 100 rounds–and some shooters report pain and discomfort after shooting far fewer shots from an extremely small or light gun–is not a gun with which you can truly master the skill of shooting accurately. Avoid buying a super lightweight handgun unless you own a nearly identical larger, heavier version with which to train and practice.

HOW MUCH IS YOUR LIFE WORTH?

There is one last aspect of handgun selection that we must address. It is not comfortable, because we all know it is not polite to discuss another person's finances. Still, we can't argue that people of all economic means need handguns for personal protection, and in fact, those of modest income often live in areas that are plagued by violent crime, further increasing their need for a reliable, effective means of self defense. Even if you are firmly in the middle-class, the pressures of balancing the house payment, the car payment, and all the other needs of a family, makes pulling $450-$850 out of the budget for a handgun purchase pretty challenging.

There are handguns sold for $200-$350. Most are an unwise investment, and these low-cost models are rarely as reliable, durable, well finished or user friendly as a more expensive handgun. If you decide you absolutely must compromise on a low-cost handgun, at least make sure it is chambered in a solid, self-defense caliber, and that it functions with 100 percent reliability. Your very safety depends on this decision, so before making this compromise, invest considerable time in comparison shopping to be sure the "deal" you are considering is really a good value.

If you invest some effort, you may instead find a gently-used handgun that has come back to the gun shop as a trade in or that is being sold on consignment by someone who decided it was not entirely suitable for his or her needs. Some worries attach to buying a used handgun, and you have to ask, "Why does the former owner want to dispose of this gun? Does it function reliably?" If it is possible to test fire the gun, buy a box of ammunition and put that concern to rest. Unfortunately, test firing is rarely allowed unless you are purchasing a gun from a private party with whom you can make plans to meet at a local firing range.

There are other guidelines for buying used guns, but with our focus on concealed carry, this is not the place to cover those in detail. Research books and articles about buying used guns if you believe this is the best route for you. You may find a starting place on a website that I manage for the Armed Citizens' Legal Defense Network, Inc. Two gunsmiths contributed articles on buying used guns to our online journal, and you can download PDFs of these articles from the April 2008 editions on the webpage http://armedcitizensnetwork.org/our-journal?start=42

Like Goldilocks in the bears' home, the four-inch barreled S&W Model 686 at the top of the stack is probably too big for concealed carry. The Airweight snub-nosed Model 642 at the bottom is probably too small and way too light for extensive shooting, while the S&W Model 60 in stainless steel with a three-inch barrel often turns out to be "just right." All are fitted with CrimsonTrace Laser Grips.

SETTING YOUR PRIORITIES

Maybe it would be easier if only one kind and model of handgun was manufactured. Of course, that is a joke, because not only do people come in a variety of sizes, people also have a number of different needs and their abilities are extremely divergent. We'd be pretty unhappy if there was only one kind of automobile available, say a mid-sized sedan painted blue with seats, steering wheel and mirrors welded into fixed and non-adjustable positions. Such a car might be entirely suitable for a few, but for many, it would fail in a number of serious ways! The same is true of handguns, and with a free market system that is driven by the purchasing public, handgun manufacturers keep bringing out new models and updating existing models every year. How is a woman to choose? You could start by making a list of your priorities. It will probably look something like this:

1. Functions reliably
2. Effective caliber for self defense
3. User friendly and adequately outfitted for self-defense use (This requires answers to questions like, "Are the sights and controls like the magazine release big enough to use under stress?")
4. Grips are big enough to attain a good shooting grip
5. Heavy enough to soak up recoil
6. Durable enough that you can practice and train with it to develop a high level of shooting skill and practice enough to maintain those skills
7. Brand and model is in current production and commonly used by a goodly number of shooters so that repairs, holsters, accessories and aftermarket products are readily available

---

(1) The Farnam Method of Defensive Handgunning, John S. Farnam, 2nd edition, 2005, ISBN-13: 978-0965942249. More information at http://www.defense-training.com/bookshelf.html

(2) http://www.gundigest.com/

FITTING YOUR CONCEALED CARRY HANDGUN

You can save money and a lot of inconvenience if, before buying a handgun, you understand proper handgun fit and why fitting a gun to your hand is critical to your skill as a shooter. Before settling on a specific handgun for your concealed carry needs, you need to understand the interface between your hand and your handgun. "How hard can that be?" someone asks. "Don't you just put your hand on the grips and close your fingers around it? Don't you just put your finger on the trigger and pull it?"

Ergonomics is a science that studies how to fit equipment to humans for the most efficient use. Knowledge from ergonomics studies is used by gun manufacturers, who design and produce firearms based on what the studies determine is an average-sized human hand. In handguns, the ergonomics–that is, shape and design of the gun and its controls–take into consideration not only the overall size of the handgun, but the angle at which the grip is offset from the barrel, the size and shape of the grip, and the distance from the backstrap to the trigger face, to name only the top concerns. Other ergonomic factors, of course, influence how easily or naturally the human hand accesses the various controls–the slide stop/slide release lever, the magazine release, the safety and the decocker used to safely lower a semi-auto pistol's hammer to double action, for example.

The complicating factor, of course, is that there is no single, uniform hand size or shape. While most hands consist of four fingers and a thumb, the depth and breadth of the palm varies, as does the length and thickness of the fingers, the hand's strength and flexibility, and even funny details like the length of the thumb in relationship to the other digits. As a result, a handgun that is a perfect fit for a shooting champion or for your best shooting buddy may fail abysmally for you.

In slow-fire target shooting, humans demonstrate amazing adaptability to overcome poor gun fit and even with terrible equipment many folks find ways to shoot accurately. In the heat of a life-and-death struggle, however, we rely much more upon the fit of the gun to accommodate fast aiming and to aid trigger control when much more is at stake than winning a championship or bragging rights for a tight shot group.

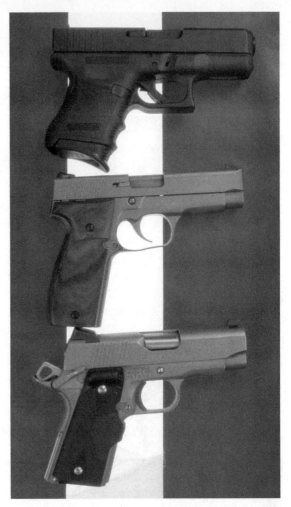

Three common handguns demonstrate the differences in trigger reach, ranging from (top to bottom) the huge Glock Model 30, the small-hand friendly Kahr T9 (Tactical 9mm), and the Springfield Armory Officer's Model with an extremely short after-market trigger installed.

When shooting, finger position on the trigger is vital to trigger control. If pressed with only the tip of the finger, the trigger pull may be too stiff for the shooter to overcome, and they may be unable to smoothly apply pressure until the gun discharges. Without allowing the trigger finger a good purchase on the trigger, in the struggle to move the trigger through its stroke, the shooter will probably pull the muzzle off target so the shot is inaccurate. Shooters are best able to smoothly manipulate the trigger by placing the crease of the trigger finger's first joint squarely on the face of the trigger when the handgun is centered in the web of the hand and gripped high on the backstrap. If possible, buy a gun on which the trigger reach measurement is short enough for you to accomplish this reach. Alternately, you may be able to modify the gun or change its grips to achieve this hand position when firing the gun.

Some will try to achieve better leverage on the trigger by moving the hand down on the grips. This is a bad idea because it creates a pivot point that lets the muzzle rise unimpeded during recoil. For maximum recoil control and fastest shot-to-shot times, the web of the hand needs to be jammed up tight against the grip tang on a semi-auto, or as high up on the backstrap of a revolver as it can be without running into the hammer when it comes back during the trigger pull.

When the shooter's hands are too small and the handgun can't be modified to shorten the trigger reach, the shooter has to use an offset grip to attain proper finger position on the trigger during shooting. The backstrap of the handgun is

The Smith & Wesson M&P pistol's adjustable backstraps give the shooter grip size options that determine how much trigger finger reach she enjoys. Castings demonstrate the different fit and show how much finger contacts the trigger when comparing their large and small options.

Glock's 4th Generation pistols, seen here in the Model 22 iteration, start with a small grip (UPPER) to which two additional grip inserts can be added to increase grip size, with the largest size shown here (LOWER).

Burns Custom Glock grip reduction (shown left and right) gives much better trigger reach for smaller hands than the straight-from-the-factory Glock 23 grip (middle).

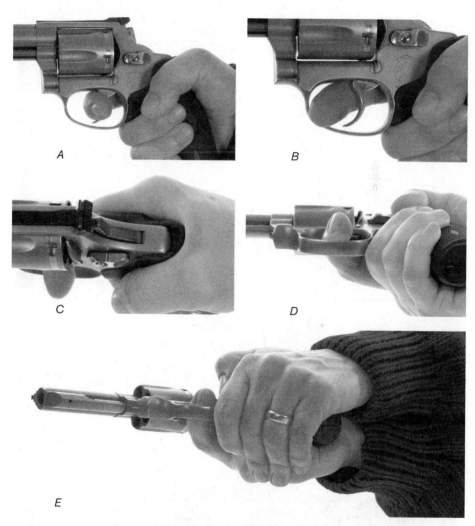

A

B

C

D

E

Seen from various aspects, we are able to analyze the proper grip and trigger reach for a revolver. A) This familiar angle shows a strong grip on the Model 60 five-shot revolver. B) As the finger goes to the trigger, we can see the crease of the first distal joint, as it prepares to curl around the trigger. C) Seen from above, the grips of the revolver are snugged deeply into the web of the hand, so deeply that there is none of the grip visible above the palm's web. D) Viewed from below, we see how the trigger finger engages the trigger at the first distal joint, when the grips and gun are perfectly fit to the shooter's hand. E) We prefer to use a two handed grip whenever possible, and in this view from below, we see how the support hand dovetails over the knuckles of the primary hand.

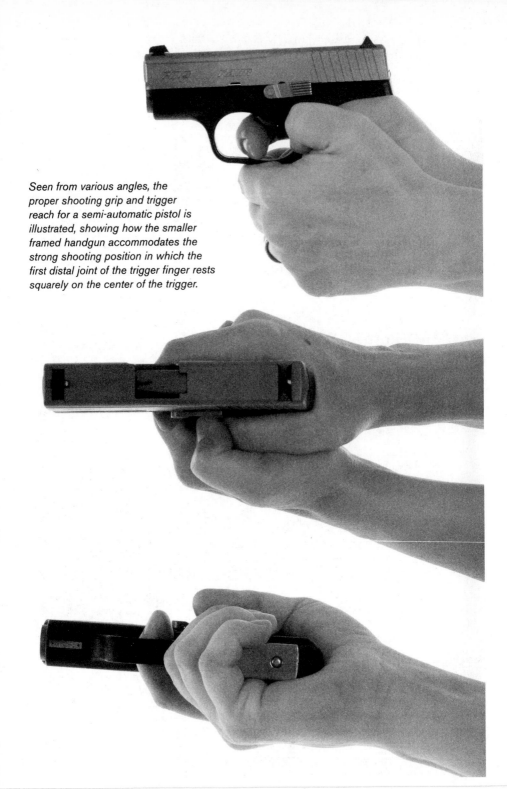

Seen from various angles, the proper shooting grip and trigger reach for a semi-automatic pistol is illustrated, showing how the smaller framed handgun accommodates the strong shooting position in which the first distal joint of the trigger finger rests squarely on the center of the trigger.

As an instructor and student discuss grip, the instructor points out the void created by not taking a high grip...

...and by lifting beneath the barrel demonstrates how there is nothing to stop the muzzle rise under recoil.

When the student takes a proper grip, the instructor can show how recoil cannot lever the muzzle up, because the web of the student's hand prevents the movement.

Smaller hands with a larger gun shoot best in the offset grip, seen here from various angles.

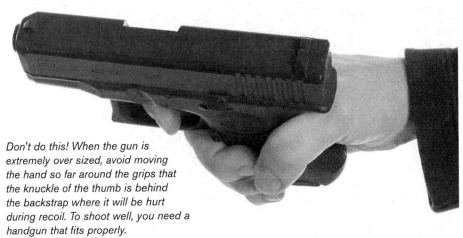

Don't do this! When the gun is extremely over sized, avoid moving the hand so far around the grips that the knuckle of the thumb is behind the backstrap where it will be hurt during recoil. To shoot well, you need a handgun that fits properly.

moved off the center of the hand's web and toward the base of the thumb until more of the trigger finger can contact the face of the trigger. This hand adjustment must never be taken so far that the backstrap contacts the thumb joint or worse, is atop it, since the recoil of firing the gun against the joint is at first uncomfortable then painful, and eventually can damage the joint by bringing on premature arthritis.

GRIP AND STANCE VARIATIONS

When you go to the shooting range, you may notice a variety of gripping methods and different upper and lower body positions in use by the other shooters. Success at the various shooting disciplines imposes different handgun and shooting method requirements and these are reflected in stance, grip and other details. You will see techniques employed specifically to win at competitive shooting when there is no danger of an aggressive assailant attempting to take your gun away, for example. In addition, you will also see very stylized foot and leg positions that do not accommodate the necessity of movement that is inherent in a defensive situation, which may entail retreat to safety or rushing to move a loved one out of harm's way—with a gun in your hand and possibly while firing that gun.

It is important to understand these distinctions, because when you carry a gun for defense, you need to be able to move and shoot, you need to grip the gun in a way that is least vulnerable to disarming, and you need to be able to shoot accurately with a good balance of speed and precision, a concept that Rob Pincus[1] has defined very well. Defense against disarms calls for a double-fisted grip on the gun when circumstances allow two-handed shooting, and the strongest possible one-fisted grip when shooting one handed, as may be required if one hand is injured or occupied with a critical task like carrying a child.

Other competition affectations influence position of the trigger finger on the trigger, since a sport that is entirely focused on extreme accuracy uses firearms with very light trigger pull weight for minimal disruption of sight alignment when the shooter exerts the lightest possible pressure with the tip of the finger to discharge the gun. Conversely, guns that are set up for personal protection need heavier trigger pull weights, preferably no lighter than five or six pounds, as a margin of safety against discharging the gun prematurely or unintentionally during the extreme stress of defending against attack or imminent attack. One of the symptoms of being in a freeze-fight-flee state is reduced sensation in the extremities, as the body prepares for the possibility of injury. With less tactile feedback from your fingertips, it is essential that your defense gun's trigger pull weight requires a noticeable amount of effort to discharge the gun. The opposite is a formula for disaster.

Sometimes shooters and instructors who are deep into competitive shooting will talk about gripping the handgun lightly, with 60 percent of the gripping pressure coming from the primary hand and 40 percent from the support hand. Conversely, I think we have to pursue a balance between how we deliver our most rapid and accurate gunfire and what the human body can perform under the stress of a life-and-death attack, and that means we will simply grip

Not just your average loving American couple! Tom and Diane Walls practice disarm responses, with Tom acting as the "bad guy," and Diane demonstrating handgun retention techniques to keep an assailant from taking her handgun.

the handgun with all of our strength. Effectively using a handgun when life is on the line relies on skills learned, practiced and habituated through repetition, coupled with techniques that humans can perform when adrenaline is pumping and fractions of seconds can mean the difference between living and dying.

NATURAL POINT OF AIM

You may have heard the term "natural point of aim" discussed primarily in relationship to how angled the shooter's body is to the target, and particularly in reference to rifle shooting. As taught for slow fire pursuits like bench rest riflery, angling the body to attain natural point of aim from a static shooting position is all but irrelevant to defending against a close-quarters attack with handguns at real life speeds where both defender and assailant move around. We can, however, learn grip and stance techniques that position the hands, arms and upper body to naturally align the gun's barrel with the center of the target as the shooter faces it. This aspect of the shooting stance is not uniform for all shooters, since that the relationship between the shape and size of the shooter's hands and the size of their gun is a little different for everyone.

Because humans come with variously-sized hands, differences in grip circumference and trigger reach help each find guns that work well. The very large Glock Model 30 fits well in Frank's large hands, while the far smaller Glock Model 26 is actually a little too big in Gila's. (TOP) The Glock Model 30 is so large that it is unreasonable to try to adapt Gila's grip and stance to fit it. (BELOW)

Grip and stance adaptations help achieve natural pointing despite different trigger reach measurements. Small grips and small hands give natural pointability in the Weaver stance, which the author achieves with a small grip on an Officer's Model 1911 (TOP) for a most natural point of aim. This is because in the Weaver stance, we align the barrel of the gun with the bones of the forearm, as is illustrated here. (LEFT)

As discussed earlier, if the gun is just a bit too big, it is preferable to move the backstrap off the center of the web of the hand toward the thumb's base so that the trigger finger starts its work from the strongest-possible position from which to pull the trigger. If, because of a slightly oversized gun, you find that you need to use an offset grip, when you lock your arm straight out, perpendicular from the shoulder, to bring the pistol up to eye level to aim, the gun's barrel is inevitably canted several degrees off from your body's center line. In other words, a right-handed shooter using an offset grip will naturally point the gun

The larger grip and frame of a Glock Model 23 coupled with the Isosceles stance, however, will point very naturally into the center of the target with use of an offset grip in hands the size of Gila's. Naturally, with larger hands, the equation is different. The large-framed Glock 30 works well in the Weaver stance in Frank's extra-large hands (BOTTOM RIGHT).

a little to the right; a lefty will find the sights out of alignment a little to the left. The further offset the grip, the greater this discrepancy becomes.

How much of a problem is it if small hands and a large gun mean the gun comes up on target pointing off center, that is, it does not point naturally for you? Just take a good look at the sight picture, pull the sights back into alignment and soldier on, right? That sounds good in theory or when shooting without time constraints gives you time to keep realigning the sights. Under the dynamic conditions of an assault, however, if you are working through conditions of bad lighting, compromised vision, on a moving target or if you are shooting while moving toward safety, adjusting gun position to attain sight alignment is very difficult. Does this mean that a small-handed shooter who simply cannot find a handgun with a short enough trigger reach is doomed? Of course not! It does mean, though, that we may need to alter our upper body shooting stance to counteract that outboard angle, if using the offset grip to attain better trigger contact on a slightly oversized handgun.

When shooting with an offset grip, the barrel will align on a target squarely in front of you most naturally when you take a two-handed grip on the gun and thrust it straight out centered in front of your face. This natu-rally angles the wrist as you straighten your arms and lock the elbows. This position has been quantified as the Isosce-les shooting stance and enjoys a considerable following. It's fast, and it is very natural to the stress reaction of squar-ing to the target and leaning forward to fight.

The other circumstance in which the Isosceles shoot-ing stance is particularly ap-plicable is when the shooter's dominant hand is not on the

The Isosceles stance viewed from right, left and top.

When a gun with a shorter trigger reach is partnered with the smaller handed shooter, the Weaver Stance makes the most of the hand and arm's natural pointing instinct.

same side as her dominant eye, a condition described as cross-dominance. When facing this situation, it makes sense to fit yourself with a gun that requires you to shoot in a slightly offset grip so you can use natural point of aim for when it is hard to see the sights, plus the advantage of that natural point of aim positioning the sights naturally in front of your eyes for the times when lighting allows or a small or distant target requires accurate sight use.

When the shooter has a smaller gun or larger hands, it makes sense to take full advantage of the natural pointing that occurs by lining the gun barrel up with the bones of the forearm. To do this, we angle the gun-side shoulder slightly away from the target so that the arm can lock out straight and maximize that natural point of aim that runs from our dominant eye, to down the dominant side arm, over a straight, locked wrist, to the pistol sights and thence to the target.

In this position, the support arm will need to be slightly bent and should pull back against outward pressure of the gun arm, which gives a very strong, recoil-controlling platform from which to deliver multiple shots rapidly. Traditionally, this shooting stance is known as the modified Weaver position, or if both arms are bent, the Weaver shooting stance.

When conditions deteriorate and we become more dependent on point shooting or employ the alternative aiming methods addressed in Chapter 6, *Just Learning to Shoot*, hits will go in the direction in which the gun barrel naturally points, so it is important to tailor our shooting grip and stance to match our handgun fit to achieve the best possible natural aiming.

Rarely does the influence of hand-to-gun size on stance make it into a defensive handgun class, where it is more common for an instructor to be heavily invested in the benefits of one shooting stance over another. Unfortunately, students never arrive at class uniformly sized or carrying guns of identical dimensions. When, after our director Marty Hayes quantified these concepts, we began teaching these stance modifications at the Firearms Academy of Seattle,[2] our students' success in the low light shooting skills taught from beginning, intermediate and advanced skill levels skyrocketed. No longer were many of the students working against their natural point of aim. Each student was, instead, being guided

Kahr Arms models T9, and PM9 accommodate small hands perfectly, showing us how grip length and barrel length is inconsequential to gun fit, but the measurement from the backstrap to the face of the trigger and the girth of the grips is critical.

to take greatest advantage of the way their gun naturally pointed in their own hand. Hits to the center of the target delivered in very limited light showed the validity of Hayes' conclusions about hand-to-gun fit and its influence on the shooting stance used.

Now, I realize that the last page or two has read a bit like a master's thesis. Here's the bottom line: most women have smaller hands than that mythical average man for whom handguns are designed. This size discrepancy has been quantified as being as much as a full digit on the trigger finger shorter for most women. That means that if you don't buy a handgun with a short trigger reach like a single-action semi-automatic or Kahr Arms' marvelously small handguns, buying instead in the uber-reliable Glock pistol or Smith & Wesson M&P lines for example, you will probably enjoy the best natural point of aim using an offset grip.

So long as you can keep the gun's backstrap off your thumb knuckle, shooting in an offset grip should pose no problems whatsoever. Using this stance advantage will greatly expand the handgun choices from which small-handed shooters can select a perfect concealed carry gun with which to shoot accurately in a variety of situations.

Inversely, if you have long fingers and a larger hand, or you select a handgun with a very short trigger reach, you owe it to yourself to experiment with the modified Weaver stance to get the most natural pointability and recoil control out of lining up the gun barrel with the bones in your forearm. Neither stance has a particular advantage over the other, but knowing which grip and stance

Brand name does not indicate gun size. The author can shoot the Glock Model 23 (TOP) using an offest grip in Isosceles stance, but the Model 30 (BOTTOM) is so large she cannot reach the trigger properly even in an offset grip.

Common semi-auto handguns like the Model 1911, which is made by a variety of manufacturers, also comes in a tremendous variety of sizes from the five-inch barreled full size down through the Officer's Model subcompact and the super compact mini like the Sig Sauer P938 shown at the left. Most can be further modified with relative ease to fit a shorter trigger, to reduce the size of the grips, or to add functionality, as in the case of these Crimson Trace LaserGrips on a Springfield Armory's 9mm Officer's Model. (BOTTOM)

Step by step demo of Jim Cirillo's method to fit the shooter's grip to her handgun. After triple checking to be sure gun is unloaded by pushing a finger into the magazine well to prove there is no magazine inside, then probing the empty chamber to feel the edges of the chamber assuring yourself there is no cartridge of ammunition chambered, close the action and place trigger finger crease on the trigger first. (TOP LEFT) *Wrap hand around the pistol in a proper, high shooting grip.* (TOP RIGHT) *Is any part of the gun's frame contacting the proximal knuckle of the thumb?* (BOTTOM RIGHT) *This will create problems, so seek a smaller gun.*

gives you the best pointing characteristics with your own handgun is important to advancing your shooting skills.

In the next chapters, we will turn our focus to specific handguns that may work well for concealed carry for you, while illustrating operating characteristics that you can seek out as you shop for a gun to carry. As you take this knowledge into the gun store prior to buying a gun, remember that often you can adjust for hand-gun misfits to a surprising degree, but eventually that flexibility ends at the point at which you can no longer position the gun's backstrap in the hand's web to the inside of the thumb knuckle while still contacting the trigger face with the first crease of your trigger finger. If the gun is so large for your hand that you cannot attain this fit, you will need to either change out the grips for a smaller pair, pay a gunsmith to attempt a grip reduction or simply buy a smaller gun.

---

(1) Rob Pincus, author of Combat Focus Shooting. 8725 Youngerman Ct., Ste. 305, Jacksonville, FL, 32244, 866-626-8273 http://www.icetraining.us/CF_Books.html or call 855-468-4789

(2) The Firearms Academy of Seattle, P. O. Box 400, Onalaska, WA 98570, 360-978-6100 www.firearmsacademy.com

REVOLVERS FOR CONCEALED CARRY

To better appreciate revolvers, let's undertake a brief exploration of the specific revolvers sold, their various options, and what to expect from them.

The general operating principal behind the revolver has been around since before 1836 when Samuel Colt patented the first handgun to fire from chambers in a revolving cylinder. Of course, the double-action revolvers we carry for personal protection today look and function a lot differently and are considerably more sophisticated than that early single-action revolver, the production of which even predated metallic cartridge ammunition.

In spite of that impressive timeline, don't let anyone tell you that revolvers are too old-fashioned for you to carry for self defense. You need only look at the varieties of revolvers currently manufactured to realize that the double-action revolver remains a popular option for self defense. From earlier chapters, you will remember that when selecting revolvers for self defense, we stick with the double-action operating system, since the additional step of having to manually cock a single-action revolver's hammer is too slow and too fumble-prone for defensive shooting, and the one-at-a-time reloading the single action requires is also a detriment. The very simplicity of shooting the double-action revolver is the key to its continuing popularity.

Double-action revolvers come in all sizes, from palm-sized models with five-round cylinders and two- or sub-two-inch barrels up to substantial eight-shot revolvers with six- or eight-inch barrels! Your goal is to select a carry gun that promotes accurate shooting and fast reloading, in a size that you can realistically conceal. That decision varies considerably based on your individual size, build and mode of dress.

You may be among those fortunate to be large enough and have sufficient latitude in wardrobe that a three-inch or four-inch barreled six-shot revolver is a suitable daily carry choice. Other women of smaller or thinner build, however, may find that the larger grip and the thickness of the six-shot cylinder create a noticeable bulge beneath even loose clothing, because the barrel length isn't the

(RIGHT TO LEFT) *Smith &Wesson's models 625, 686, 60 and 642 illustrate some of the various sizes of revolvers, with the Model 625 built on a larger frame, the 686 on a mid-sized frame, and the models 60 and 642 on the small frame option. These are sometimes called N, L and J frames, with the initials merely providing an identification scheme used by Smith & Wesson.*

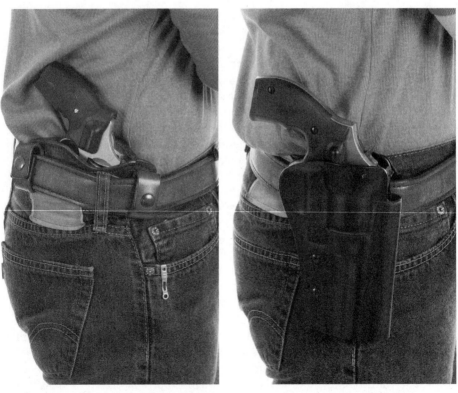

The three-inch barreled Model 60 conceals well in a custom-made IWB holster by Chris Cunningham. (LEFT) The K-framed model 686 in an outside the waistband holster would require much bulkier clothing to conceal (RIGHT) and although an IWB would help some, the larger six-shot cylinder, and larger grips just make it harder to hide.

difficult part to conceal. The longer barrel, however, can be more laborious to draw unless you are tall or the holster sits quite low.

It might seem that the five-shot revolver with a two-inch barrel, called a "snubby," is the one remaining choice. Not so! I really prefer a three-inch barreled five-shot revolver, because the barrel length is a negligible consideration for concealment, since the grips and the round cylinder are the elements that usually show through clothing. The additional weight soaks up the recoil of the discharging ammunition, and the distance between the sights (called sight radius) makes sight alignment quicker and easier. That's why for a carry revolver, one of my all-time favorites is a steel-framed Smith & Wesson Model 60 with adjustable sights and a three-inch barrel, with subtle customization by gunsmith Grant Cunningham, author of *The Gun Digest Book of the Revolver*.[1]

The three-inch barreled five-shot is not so heavy that it cannot be comfortably carried in a well-made holster, because barrel length is not usually the deciding factor in gun concealability. Carried in a belt holster, the length of the barrel simply follows the line of the hip; if anything sticks out to compromise concealment, it is the grips.

Grant Cunningham Custom Model 60 with three-inch barrel is a joy to shoot.

Gunsmith Grant Cunningham's daily carry option, a lightly customized 2-inch barreled Colt Detective.

SHOPPING BY BRAND

When double-action revolver shopping, you will become familiar with brand names including Smith & Wesson, Ruger, Taurus, Charter Arms, Rossi, and maybe even Chiappa for double-action revolvers currently in production. The Chiappa revolver is of such unique design that, unless you are an avid gun collector, it might be best to leave this imaginative revolver redesign to the collectors. Though a number of small-framed Colt double-action revolvers (which sadly ceased production in 1995) are still in circulation, the frequency with which they are showing up in the used gun display at even large gun stores is diminishing, and as a result, finding a holster or after market grips for a Colt Detective is a tall order, indeed.

Renowned revolver smith Grant Cunningham, who we've referenced earlier, earned his early reputation repairing and making custom refinements to his customers' Colts. When I asked him whether Colt revolvers were still a good choice for concealed carry, he had a lot to say on the topic, and it is instructive, not only as it tells us about this iconic brand, but on the larger question of choosing a rare handgun for daily concealed carry. Let's see what he had to say—

Cunningham explains that the Colt Detective Special (DS), produced from late 1927-1986 and again briefly in the early 1990s, was "particularly prized for concealed carry because of the six-shot cylinder in a frame scarcely larger than what Smith & Wesson had on their five-shot guns. They were also well regarded for their accuracy." In addition, the Detective Special fit small hands very well, especially with grips featuring an open backstrap, he adds.

"There were two variants of the DS made with a lightweight aluminum frame called the Cobra and the Agent. For all intents and purposes they can be considered identical and, save for weight, the same as a DS. Recoil with these very light revolvers is not for the squeamish, however," he warns. In addition, you may find used a Colt SF-VI model, which is of the same size frame as a Detective Special, but manufactured in stainless steel and using a slightly different internal mechanism, which Cunningham explains "was easier to manufacture and repair than the tightly-fitted Detective Special." The SF-VI was later renamed the DS-II. In the same frame size, you may find used models of Colt's Magnum carry, on which he notes, "Colt strengthened the SF-VI/DS-II frame, lengthened the cylinder to take .357 Magnum ammunition, and introduced it as the Magnum Carry. This gun was produced only in 1999; Colt dropped it, along with all their other double-action revolvers, in the year 2000. Magnum Carry revolvers are quite rare and command considerable collector interest."

"The big downside with all of the Colts becomes clear when they need maintenance or repair," Cunningham warns. "The Detective Special, Agent and Cobra use what is referred to as the 'old' Colt lockwork, which was designed at a time when people didn't shoot their guns a lot, labor was cheap, and there was a skilled gunsmith on nearly every street corner. The old-style Colt action demands strict maintenance and immediate attention of a gunsmith when they start to wear."

> *"There are no new parts being manufactured, and new-old-stock parts are very rare."*

Modestly failing to mention his own work, Cunningham adds, "Today such gunsmiths are hard to come by, and parts–even though the gun was manufactured for decades–are getting very scarce. There are no new parts being manufactured, and new-old-stock parts are very rare." I have known Cunningham to scour used parts catalogs for long hours seeking out parts for a challenging repair job, so there is no doubt that his assertion is verifiable.

"The newer guns–SF-VI/DS-II and Magnum Carry–suffer from similar issues with parts availability, but in this case largely because they weren't made for an extended period and didn't sell all that well. Factory parts are no longer made, and there are very few guns in the wild that can be used as parts donors. The common wear parts, like the hand, which turns the cylinder, can be hard to find. The few gunsmiths who will work on them do so primarily because they bought stocks of common spare parts when the guns were discontinued, but even those are now running out," Cunningham explains.

Still, he has an unshakable love for these old revolvers. "The Colt revolvers have quite a lot going for them, and their small size with six-shot capacity remains unique in modern handguns. (Taurus and Rossi have since made similar sized revolvers with six-shot cylinders, but quality control issues have kept them from being widely sold.) That being said, the small frame Colts should really be considered enthusiasts' guns, suitable for those who a) won't shoot them very much and b) are willing to put up with the maintenance and repair issues they present," he concludes.

Likewise, you may run across an old, used revolver that bears the Iver Johnson or Harrington & Richardson marque, but these are no longer in current production, and you'll be best off to leave them for a collector to enjoy. When I queried my friend Clay Whitehead, who is such an avid collector of antique guns in odd calibers that we call him the Keeper of the Relics, about buying old, used guns, he not only echoed Cunningham's advice to avoid out of production handguns, but added that in his career as a gun store clerk he observed considerable difficulty in obtaining repairs or parts for guns of foreign manufacture.

"My recommendation is to stay with currently available, popular calibers like .38 Special, .357, 9mm, .40 S&W, .45 ACP with .380 in there someplace. There are many really nice pistols and revolvers in some of the less available calibers (like my Walther PP in .32 ACP), but ammunition availability for both defensive ammo and practice ammo is vitally important. The handgun that you can only get one box of hardball for isn't a good choice. Current models in established brands are the recommendation," he concluded.

Cunningham and Whitehead give good advice! Since our goal is to carry a reliable gun for which we can enjoy a good selection of holsters and a reliable commercial ammunition supply, it is best to stick to popular handguns that are in current production and of a sufficiently long history that their longevity is assured.

DESIRABLE FEATURES

Beyond good hand fit, what features are desirable in a revolver for concealed carry? "Better sights!" This is always the resounding answer to that question. A lot of small-framed revolvers are outfitted with only a groove on the top strap to serve as a rear sight. The groove terminates in a square notch, the interior edges of which are used to align the front sight inside the notch just as we do when a more traditional rear pistol sight is installed. Unfortunately, the notch and groove rear sight is also quite small, which makes its use more difficult, and this is particularly true when the revolver is nickel-plated, made of stainless steel or another light colored alloy that can be hard to see clearly in bright lighting. The alternative is the more fragile and somewhat snag-prone adjustable sights. Recently, Smith & Wesson has pioneered improved contoured revolver sights that show a real understanding of the deficiencies of the ordinary fixed sights integral to most revolvers. In addition, fiber optic front sights have really changed the game.

You'll find it worth the time to shop until you find a revolver that is equipped with good sights, and it is well worth the expense to buy a revolver with a decent set of sights already installed or if necessary pay a gunsmith to upgrade your revolver's sights. In addition, laser sights make an excellent enhancement for revolvers, though I do not believe they will ever entirely replace traditional sights.

As mentioned earlier, concealment is most often compromised not by a longer barrel, but by the outline of the gun's grips printing through the covering

A variety of revolver sights: XS Sights® big dot tritium front sight installed by Smith & Wesson is used with a notch rear sight milled into the top of the receiver (LEFT). Dovetailed rear and front sight with self-luminous tritium inserts on Smith & Wesson Model 640 revolver are a far cry from the minimalist sights often milled into the top strap of many revolvers (BELOW LEFT). S&W Model 642 airweight snub nosed revolver is representative of the most common type of revolver sights, which are a front sight blade and rear sight notch milled from the same material as the frame of the gun. (BELOW RIGHT)

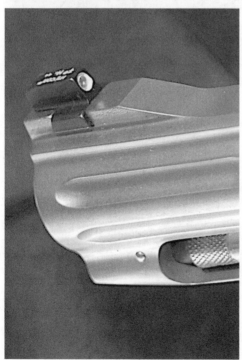

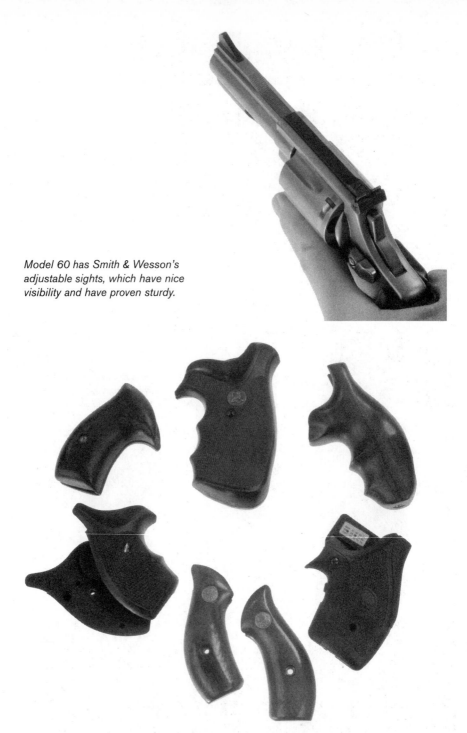

Model 60 has Smith & Wesson's adjustable sights, which have nice visibility and have proven sturdy.

Revolver replacement grips come in all sizes, shapes, colors and materials to make the grip slicker, softer, larger, smaller, shorter, longer, contoured to fit the fingers of the shooter's hand, or add functionality like the Crimson Trace LaserGrip at the lower right.

Changing revolver grips starts by having the right tools, like this Brownell's screwdriver set.

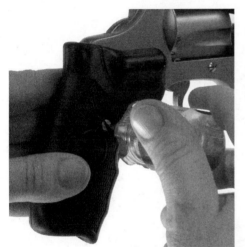

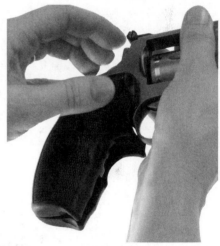

First, remove the currently installed grips.

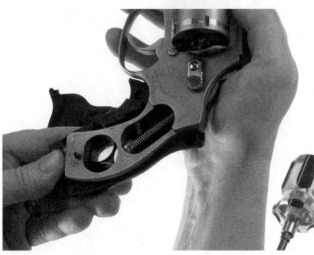

RIGHT: *Sometimes changing grips will show where better cleaning is needed, as revealed by the rust that starts beneath these grips where the hands' moisture seeps in during shooting.*

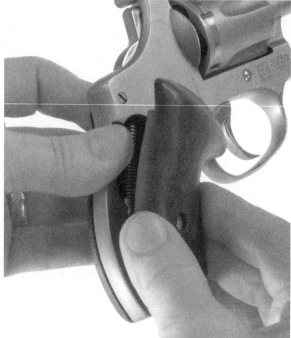

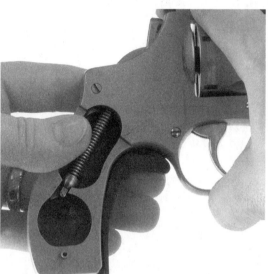

ABOVE AND RIGHT: *Fitting a new set of grips entails matching the grip fittings to pins on the revolver frame.*

clothing. Changing the grips on most revolvers is quite easy, and it's something that revolver owners frequently do to help better fit the grip to their hand, in addition to enhancing concealment or shooting comfort. If the revolver ships from the factory with grips that extend a long way below the end of the grip frame, or are of such soft rubber that your concealment clothing gets stuck on it and rides up, you can replace them, too.

You may run across the replacement grips that include a hook to catch over the waistband in lieu of a holster. We knew this concept several decades ago as the Barami Hip Grip; it has resurfaced recently as the DeSantis Gunhide® Clip-Grip™. DeSantis gets kudos for honesty when they write, "the Clip-Grip™ can be used as a comfortable alternative to a holster, but is not recommended for use while engaged in fast-paced physical activity." The break with reality, in my opinion, is that defensive shootings rarely occur in a vacuum. The need to draw

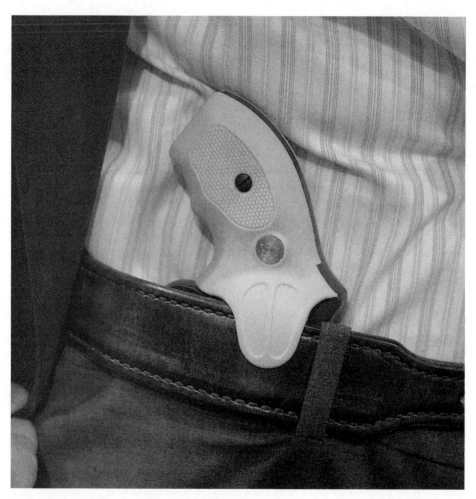

DeSantis Clip Grip®, the modern iteration of the Barami hip grip, is wide enough to hook over a belt or perhaps a thick elasticized waistband as you might have on a pair of sweatpants.

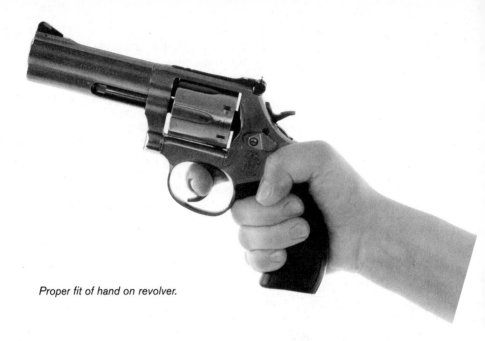

Proper fit of hand on revolver.

a gun to stop an assailant may well be preceded by "fast-paced physical activity," be that running away or grappling with an assailant to disengage, get away, or get access to reach your handgun. It is fabulously convenient for someone who doesn't carry a gun on body during all their waking hours, but before installing a holster-less carry option, we need to take an honest look at why we carry a gun and understand that a fight that precedes the need to shoot may entail a physical struggle or an attempt to run away to safety.

The primary reason to replace revolver grips, though, is to tailor the fit of the gun to the size and shape of your hands. As discussed earlier, proper handgun fit accommodates full contact of the crease of the trigger finger's first distal joint on the center of the trigger when the gun's backstrap is centered in the web of the hand. This is of particular importance with the double-action revolver, because the trigger pull weights usually range between 12 and 15 pounds of pull weight distributed over about an inch of pull, often two times as stiff and heavy as many semi-auto trigger pulls. In an attempt to cushion the shooter from some of the recoil, a lot of revolver grip makers build up the grips over the grip frame's backstrap, increasing the distance the trigger finger must reach to get into the best position to smoothly press the trigger. For smaller-handed women, this means you have to choose between proper trigger finger position and centering the backstrap in the web of the hand. Both compromises affect shooting accuracy as we move beyond slow fire into shooting multiple shots at realistic defensive speeds.

Proper trigger reach takes priority, so if you have small hands you may need to move the revolver slightly toward the shooting hand's thumb knuckle and shoot in an offset grip, though first you should shop for and take advantage of the better grip position of open backstrap grip designs like Pachmayr's Com-

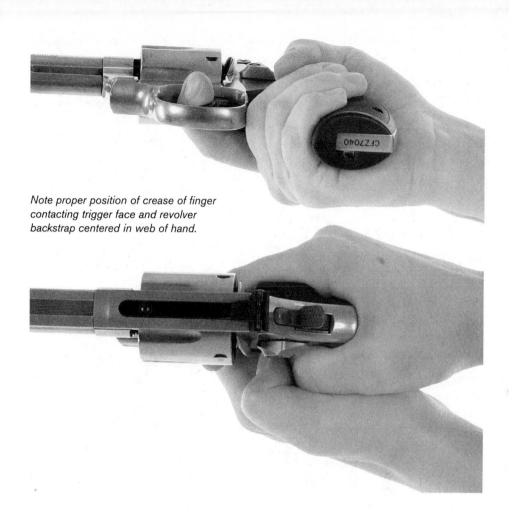

Note proper position of crease of finger contacting trigger face and revolver backstrap centered in web of hand.

When we install a larger grip that adds a lot of material to the back strap, contact between the trigger face and the trigger finger stops at the middle of the finger pad, never approaching the first joint, from which the finger and hand can give a stronger, smoother trigger pull.

Taurus revolvers have a variety of finishes, barrel lengths, caliber and grip options.

Ruger's unique LCR combines polymer frame with metal construction where necessary for a light-weight revolver.

pac Professional grips or Hogue's Bantam grips, which are only two examples of commercially available grip replacements. While grips with an open backstrap are not as comfortable during the recoil of shooting as grips with generous padding, a strong and proper grip can buffer recoil's jolt. By holding the revolver in a firm, crushing grip, properly centered in the web of the hand, we cushion against the kick of the recoil because the hard grip prevents the gun from moving jarringly during recoil. Reaching the trigger properly is more important, because what good is comfort if we cannot shoot quickly and accurately?

---

(1) DeSantis Holster & Leather Goods Co., 431 Bayview Avenue, Amityville, NY 11701, 800-GUNHIDE, http://www.desantisholster.com

(2) More information about gunsmith and author Grant Cunningham at his website http://www.grantcunningham.com

SEMI-AUTOS FOR CONCEALED CARRY

Join me in a fun exploration of some of the many semi-automatic pistols sold, summarizing their various options and how they operate, and discussing what to expect if you buy a semi-automatic handgun.

It seems that design innovation in handguns in recent years has mostly focused on semi-automatic handguns. In the previous chapter, it wasn't too taxing to list names of the major American revolver manufacturers, but the number of manufacturers–both American and foreign–offering various semi-automatic pistols to the American gun buyer is overwhelming.

As with revolvers, selecting a semi-automatic handgun from a prominent manufacturer who has a proven track record of a decade or two in business is a good idea. While everyone likes to have something that is unique, the more mainstream your defense handgun, the easier it will be for you to find a wide variety of accessories like holsters, sights, replacement magazines and grips, to say nothing of repair parts in the event of breakage.

Among semi-automatic handguns there are several discrete operating systems: single action, double action, double action only, striker fired, and some hybridization between those types. Much of the separation focuses on how the firing pin or striker is put into motion to discharge the firearm. For handguns, discharging a cartridge of ammunition is still, at present, a mechanical process by which a striker or firing pin must be released to impact the primer in the ammunition cartridge. To do so, handguns need a mechanism by which a hammer or a striker is released so it can spring or fall forward to do its work.

The single-action semi-automatic's hammer must be cocked for the gun to fire, and this is generally accomplished through cycling the slide, either manually during the initial loading sequence, or as part of the slide's cycle during firing. If practicing dryfire, the hammer can also be pulled back with a thumb. Generally, the only way to lower a single-action semi-automatic pistol's hammer (called decocking) is to press the trigger with the chamber empty.

You can manually lower the hammer, too, but there is little practical reason for doing so on a single-action semi-auto because it cannot be fired with the hammer down. There are schools of thought, the Israeli training schools, primarily, that teach to rack the slide immediately after drawing the gun, and some armed citizens have adopted this for carrying guns with the chamber empty. From my viewpoint, that is dangerous because you may not have the use of both hands as a fight progresses to the point at which you decide using deadly force to defend yourself is justifiable. Alternatively, your non-dominant hand may be occupied with securing a dependent or performing other necessary actions, and without the use of two hands, how will you quickly rack the slide to chamber a round?

Actually, it can be done, but is something I would only want to do under extreme circumstances in which I have lost the use of one hand and still need to clear a malfunction or reload. That was exactly the circumstance when Orange County Sheriff's Deputy Jennifer Fulford used one-handed reloading techniques to get back into the fight in a Florida garage, protecting herself and two children from two assailants who had shot her seven times before her Glock pistol ran dry.[1]

Still, it makes no sense to put oneself at such a disadvantage willingly, as is sometimes advocated in the name of gun safety. Many years ago, I heard the late Col. Jeff Cooper, celebrated author and founder of the Gunsite training facility, lecture on gun safety. It is important to acknowledge, he stressed, that the value of a firearm carried for self defense is found in the very fact that the gun is dangerous. If the gun was indeed not capable of causing great harm, it would be of little use in self defense. Prominent tactical instructor John Farnam echoes those sensibilities when he decries practices implemented to "make the gun safer," like carrying it without ammunition in the chamber, or other impractical attempts to mitigate its capacity to cause harm. Care must be taken not to remove the ability to act effectively in self defense, in a misguided attempt to remove all danger from our lives. As Farnam would succinctly say, "Not recommended!" Now after that diversion, let's get back to how different semi-autos operate and identify good self-defense choices.

Most single-action handguns have quite a short trigger pull, often as little as 1/8 inch, and not much pressure is required to discharge the gun. For defensive use, it is best if the trigger pull requires at least five if not six pounds to discharge the gun; extremely light trigger pulls of three to four pounds belong only on handguns used for sporting purposes, if at all.

The 1911 variant is the most common representative of the single-action semi-automatic type of handgun. These are produced by a wide variety of manufacturers, including Kimber, Smith & Wesson, Sig Sauer, Taurus, Para Ordnance, Springfield Armory, Colt, Ruger and many, many more. Less common today, but still a very attractive option, is the Hi-Power style pistol, usually sold by the Browning company. In fact, it is common to hear this type of handgun identified as the Browning Hi-Power, when actually a number of other manufacturers over the years have also produced pistols on good old John Moses Browning's Hi-Power single-action design.

Double-action semi-automatics start their firing cycle with the hammer lowered, but like the double-action revolver, pressure on the trigger both cocks

Example of a decocker in use starts by loading the Smith & Wesson Model 3913 (TOP) and racking the slide to put a round in the chamber, which also cocks the hammer. MIDDLE: A downward press on the safety/ decocking lever mechanically and safely lowers the hammer, so that the first shot will fire through trigger cocking. BOTTOM: Pulling the trigger then both cocks and releases the hammer to fire the gun, just like the double-action revolvers we discussed earlier. The firing cycle then cocks the hammer so the 3913 fires subsequent shots in single action until the decocker is used to safely lower the hammer.

The Glock and Kahr Arms pistols (RIGHT) are striker fired as is Walther's P99 (BELOW) with the striker cocked, as indicated by the protruding red dot at the back of the slide.

and releases the hammer to fire the gun. This can require from six to 15 pounds of pressure on the trigger distributed over trigger pulls of ¾ to one inch long depending on the gun's design. When the slide cycles during firing, it leaves the gun cocked so that it subsequently fires in single action, with a shorter trigger pull and pull weights of five to six pounds and lower.

The better quality examples of this gun type have additional mechanisms for safely lowering the hammer without using the trigger. These mechanisms are called decockers. Today, the most prominent manufacturer of this pistol type is Sig Sauer, though Smith & Wesson and Ruger, who once ruled this part of the market, still make a few traditional double-action semi-automatic pistols. Still, much of their product line has moved on to striker-fired pistols. Heckler & Koch, Beretta, Bersa, CZ, and Walther are other common sources for double-action autoloaders equipped with decockers.

Double-action-only guns have no single-action mode at all. Trigger pull weights and length are similar to the double-action mode of a traditional double-action pistol, and differ from traditional double-action semi-automatic operation in that every trigger pull is the same, long and often heavy, just like on a revolver. These days, most manufacturers of traditional double-action semi-autos

It is possible to manually lower a cocked hammer, as is done on this .380 ACP caliber Beretta Model 86. The procedure begins by blocking the hammer from falling forward while pressing the trigger to release it, then very carefully easing the hammer down until the gun is no longer cocked. Owing to the potential for slipping and letting the hammer fall, it is essential to have a safe backstop if ever you must attempt this procedure on a double-action semi-auto that lacks a decocking mechanism.

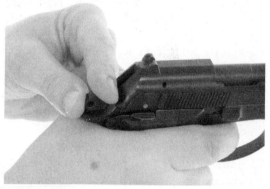

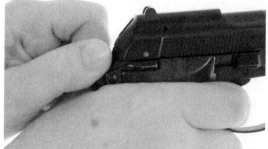

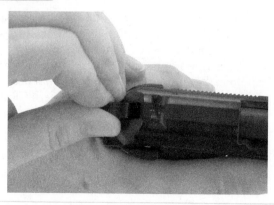

also offer variations in double-action only, usually in response to specifications required for police or military purchase bids. One unusual example is Para Ordnance's Light Double Action (LDA) model on which the length of the trigger pull is fully an inch, but the trigger pull is accomplished by applying under six pounds of pressure to the trigger, about half that of most double-action-only pistols.

Striker-fired handguns are quite similar to double-action-only semi-autos, in that every trigger pull is of the same length and weight, but the striker-fired mechanism generally requires in the neighborhood of five pounds pull weight, give or take a pound or so. Some in the gun press have gone so far as to argue that striker-fired pistols are merely light double-action only and I even read one author who purported that striker-fired pistols are classified as single-action only operation. I'd jettison the single-action or double-action nomenclature entirely, and catalog them separately, simply because the firing mechanism does not use a hammer that strikes a firing pin at all. Instead, the striker-fired gun is generally discharged when the trigger pull first cams a safety block out of the way, releasing a firing pin held under spring pressure so it can hit and spark the ammunition's primer. There are a number of variations on the striker-fired theme, all of which work a little differently, a topic that is much broader than our need to simply understand in general terms the various handgun operating systems.

Striker-fired pistols have been around for decades, but they really rose to prominence in the United States with the adoption of the Glock auto pistol by law enforcement agencies, a trend which private gun owners eagerly copied. Soon thereafter, a dozen manufacturers were offering striker-fired semi-auto pistols, including Smith & Wesson, Steyr, Kahr Arms, Walther, Heckler & Koch, Kimber, Springfield Armory, Taurus and many, many more.

OTHER OPTIONS

Beyond the different operating systems, different semi-automatic designs may or may not feature various options, like the decocking levers mentioned earlier, slide lock/release levers, as well as manual safeties, automatic or passive safeties like the in-trigger safeties that Glock has made so popular. You will also want to check to be sure the handgun you buy to carry has a passive drop safety, which is an internal block designed to prevent discharge of the firearm unless the trigger is pulled. While you cannot see this internal safety, its role is important to the overall safety of the gun, and some of the very cheap guns sold are so simple that this element is left off.

There is one more distinction between types of semi-automatic handguns that you may encounter. This is the difference between locked breech and blow back operation. Usually the shooter is not necessarily aware of any operational difference between the two. The distinction is in how the slide separates from the barrel during the ejection cycle, since the pressure of the discharging cartridge needs to drop to safe levels before the breech opens, otherwise the cartridge case would rupture. The locked breech system mechanically delays the moment at which the slide unlocks from the barrel until the bullet is out of the

Glock's in-trigger safety prevents the pistol from firing unless the center spar on the trigger is pressed. Thus, inadvertent contact with the side of the trigger is insufficient to discharge the pistol, but anything that presses against the center of the trigger face can make the gun fire.

barrel; the blow back system uses a strong spring and massive slide to accomplish the same result.

It seems that no two gun brands are exactly the same. Even magazine releases are sometimes in one or two positions, on the side of the grips adjacent to the trigger guard or to the rear at the base of the grips and only occasionally elsewhere. These variations in outfitting and in function are another good reason to start with a solid introductory handgun class where you can try a variety of handguns, then continue your experience by patronizing a shooting range with a gun rental counter where you can try before you buy a gun for concealed carry.

There exist a tremendous variety of handguns in numerous calibers, various modes of operation, a myriad of sizes and weights, and even a variety of colors. We've only scratched the surface in the last three chapters, introducing factors you will need to sort through before purchasing your own gun.

Hands-on experience is the best way to choose equipment that works for you, and while you can apply the principles we discussed in the gun fit and ergonomics chapter, only shooting a variety of guns will help you decide what really feels right in your hands. Many firearms schools and instructors offer classes for beginners that provide handguns for the students to shoot. This is a wise first step.

After completing that training, look for a gun range that rents a variety of handguns, as I have recommended. I've emphasized this option because shooting 50 to 100 rounds of ammunition through the brand and model of gun you will eventually buy is the only way to discover if there are design features that don't work well for you. The range's rental counter will generally require that you provide ID and may take other measures to protect their business from the mistake of providing a firearm to someone legally prohibited from gun possession, and you will be asked to buy ammunition you will shoot through their rental handguns from them, as well. Don't balk at either! Trying a wide variety of handguns is the best way to choose a handgun you will be able to learn to shoot well, and the rental counter at the gun range is an incredible resource you should not fail to exploit.

---

(1) Police Magazine online edition, http://www.policemag.com/blog/firearms-and-tactics/story/2010/11/pinned-down-in-a-gunfight.aspx

EMBARRASSING MOMENTS FOR ARMED WOMEN

A lot of responsibility comes with carrying a concealed handgun. Because carrying a gun adds just one more complication to our already complex lives, carrying a gun in public is a fertile breeding ground for errors that can sometimes be embarrassing and sometimes prove very dangerous. These usually center on having to handle the firearm in less than secure circumstances. How do you practice gun safety when you work in a "gun free zone," or during different recreational pursuits like water sports, for example, where the gun has to be taken off and secured before you dive in?

Go to your gun club or local indoor range and hang around the coffee pot or the soda machine. Chances are you won't even have to start the conversation, but eventually talk will turn to "most embarrassing moments" in the life of the armed citizen. These usually center on the inadvertent exposure of a concealed handgun under circumstances that were less than ideal.

Imagine that a friend makes a romantic "pass," and instead of giving you a nice warm hug, gets a handful of your Glock Model 26. A playful young child at the local playground dashes headlong into your hip and bellows in outrage, "Mommy! Your gun hurt my head!" You stand to rise from a comfortable captain-style chair at a nice restaurant when your gun's grips tangle in the chair arms, making a loud clacking sound, tipping the chair over and jerking the gun half out of its holster. We've already discussed solutions to a lot of these problems in the Chapter 5, but there are more serious errors you may hear related over coffee at the shooting range from which we can learn, too.

While the myriad stories about inadvertent breaches in concealment are instructional and funny to all but the embarrassed party, there are more serious errors of which you should be aware. These usually center on a dropped gun or a dropped magazine, or rounds of ammunition that got loose and rolled around in a public place.

You may hear of guns forgotten in backpacks that are discovered when the luggage goes through the security scanner at work or at the airport. You may hear of guns forgotten and left behind at the range or in motel rooms, or in public restrooms.

You will probably also hear tales of dropped guns. Guns that fell out of holsters when the armed citizen was rolling around on the ground; guns that fell out of waist packs when the zipper or Velcro® separated; guns, magazines or knives that clanked to the public restroom floor when the armed citizen assumed a seated position on the commode. It is instructive to recognize how often these disconcerting episodes occur in a stall in a public restroom. The blame usually goes to cheap concealment systems that inadequately secure the gun or the magazines or speed loaders, which are dislodged preparatory to using the toilet.

Some mishaps are more serious. You will sometimes hear of negligent discharges that occur when an unholstered gun becomes entangled in detritus with which it shares the pocket or purse in which the clueless gun owner carried it. That is the easiest to cure. It is dangerous to carry a loaded gun without putting it inside a properly designed holster. Don't ever do it. Even if you carry nothing else in the pocket in which you intend to put the gun, put the gun in a pocket holster first, and then put both in the pocket. Clothing isn't rigid enough to protect the trigger from inadvertent contact without the barrier of the holster to protect it.

> *It is dangerous to carry a loaded gun without putting it inside a properly designed holster. Don't ever do it.*

Purse carry is most safely practiced in one of the many fashionable bags designed specifically for concealed carry. These pretty pistol purses feature separate compartments for the gun, and the best designs include a built-in holster so that the gun is held in the same orientation all the time. Thus, when your hand reaches for the grips, they are always in the same place. The pocket holster serves the same purpose. Alessi Holsters has a clip holster that does double duty as an inside-the-waistband holster as well as a holster clipped inside the pocket of a fashionable handbag. We'll review these products in detail a bit later. For now, suffice it to say that concealed carry done safely really requires a holster.

Just any old holster won't do, though. For a holster to do its job, it has to be made specifically to fit the model of gun it carries. If it is not molded to the exact contours of the gun's trigger guard, ejection port and other topography, the holster needs a retention strap to guarantee that the gun does not fall out. The latter method is widely used in holster waist packs and gun purses. For high-quality belt holsters, the holster's material is generally molded so that the holster locks lightly around the gun when the gun is holstered. Accurate molding is one way to identify a high-quality holster. A holster that retains the gun through molding, not a strap across the top, is quicker and surer from which to draw, and more readily secures the gun if it must be holstered quickly during an incident, for example.

When carrying a gun in a belt holster, the question of how to secure it while using the toilet is quite a topic of contention. One school of thought calls for drawing the gun and setting it on the toilet tank, the tissue roll dispenser, or other flat surface. This is probably functional at home and maybe even in a locked single restroom if you're not too germ-phobic. This solution, however, is very iffy in restrooms with multiple stalls separated by metal dividers where one door slamming shakes the entire structure, and the toilets rarely have water tanks at all. Here, some trainers recommend drawing the gun and stowing it in your purse, or even in the crotch of your trousers. If the gun must come out of the holster at all, a safer solution, in my opinion, is the one offered by Kathy Jackson, author of The Cornered Cat[1] website, who recommends hanging your purse on the coat hook, opening it, and stowing the gun in the purse.

> **Accurate molding is one way to identify a high-quality holster.**

Since I have been carrying a gun for some two decades, I've honed my carry gear to such good equipment that I can hold the belt tight against my thigh and the gun and holster remain safely upright, even with the trousers lowered. I prefer this option in restrooms, since it entails absolutely NO gunhandling in a public place. My dear friend Vicki Farnam likes a purse holster for these circumstances, since, like my solution, it entails no gunhandling whatsoever.

The aspect of all this gun handing that troubles me greatly is that there is no safe gun direction in a public restroom or even a single restroom in a public building, and often a safe, bullet-stopping backstop is not available in the home restroom, either. With respect to all the folks who recommend various places to stash your gun in a public restroom, I simply will not do it. When you draw the gun out of the safety of its holster and handle it, that loaded gun is pointing somewhere. Inadvertent contact with the trigger can discharge it with very tragic results, since something important may be forward of the muzzle in the direction in which the gun points.

Again, good gear contributes much to avoiding a dangerous problem. A gun carried on a rigid belt in a holster that is molded to the shape of the gun will stay securely in the holster even when it is not in its normal, muzzle-down orientation on your waistband. Close your gun-side hand around holster, belt and waistband while lowering your trousers. If bathroom duties require both hands, squeeze the holster against the outside of your thigh until pulling your britches up. Denim jeans sometimes have enough stiffness to do this alone, but with a softer fabric like wool gabardine, you can also buckle your belt around your thighs or knees to create the needed tension, if that proves necessary. Yes, this takes some finesse, but it can be done. I've been doing it for years. That way the gun need never leave the security of the holster, where the covering over the trigger guard provides a considerable margin of safety against an unintentional and very dangerous discharge.

DANGER - FALLING OBJECTS!

Finally, before moving on from this embarrassingly personal discussion, we should discuss what to do if you drop a gun. Whether a gun is dropped on the shooting range, in your home or out in public, this rule applies: if a gun falls, let it fall, then retrieve it from the ground or floor. The danger of a high-quality, well-made gun discharging when dropped is negligble compared to the likelihood that you will get tangled up in the trigger guard and press the trigger while desperately trying to catch the gun in the air before it hits the floor. Buy a high-quality handgun and trust the internal safeties built in to prevent an inertia discharge. Internal safeties block the hammer or striker from moving forward to strike the ammunition's primer unless the trigger is first pulled, disengaging the internal safety. Do not trust your ability to snatch a falling gun from the air safely.

A gun stored inside a parked car absolutely must be secured inside an irremovable lock box.

Dropping a gun or unintentionally discharging a gun are the most serious safety breaches you must prevent through safe gun handling habits and the quality of the concealed carry system you purchase. Fortunately, if you take these issues seriously and enact safeguards to prevent negligent accidents from happening, you probably have more to worry about from the embarrassing but non-injurious mistakes a concealed carry practitioner may suffer.

The best solution to avoiding an embarrassing gun mistake is to not fiddle with your gun or magazines in public. Put them on in the morning stowed in high-quality holsters, belts and magazine pouches, and leave them in place until you undress to get into your pajamas. If you are distracted, cold, stressed to the extent that you are breathing hard or have an elevated heart rate, it is likely that you will not possess the manual dexterity needed for safe and secure gun manipulation. If at all possible, develop an ironclad routine by which you put on your concealed handgun before leaving home and do not fiddle with it until you are back home.

A job in a gun-free zone, like most schools for example, or regular appointments inside a restricted area like a courthouse, a routine that includes a daily visit to the health club swimming pool, or any other regular event that you cannot legally or safely complete while armed, will require special provisions. In these cases, you can carry your gun in a waist pack that you can secure in a locker or in a locking box that is bolted to the floorboards of your car.

A gun stored inside a parked car absolutely must be secured inside an irremovable lock box, owing to the frequency with which cars are broken into and ransacked. Products like the Shot Lock[2] or other heavy-duty options are best, since cheaply constructed lock boxes have been demonstrated, often with online video demonstrations from which any criminal can learn, to be easily pried open or otherwise defeated. As gun owners, one of our greatest responsibilities is keeping our firearms out of the hands of criminals.

When installing a lock box in your car, take into consideration where you will have the safest yet most private access to it. Avoid positioning it where you will have to point your gun at your legs or at your passenger when putting the

Truck Vault's Shot Lock is sturdily made but is small and light enough to carry from place to place if the armed citizen chooses to not use the holes manufactured in the back to bolt it to the floor of her car.

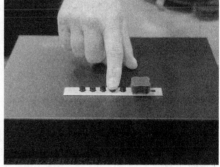

V-Line[3] has a long reputation for customer satisfaction making lock boxes for safe gun storage in the home. A Simplex-type Kaba lock is quick to use. Please use a gun safe or a heavy-duty, reliable lock box to keep your firearms out of unauthorized hands.

gun in the lock box or bringing it out. Do not leave the lockbox readily visible to strangers outside of your car. Cover it up with something a thief wouldn't want like a ratty old sweatshirt or other camouflaging item, perhaps a well-thumbed magazine, when you leave the car.

Practicing safety is nearly always a balancing act. We strive to tread the middle road between never venturing out for fear of danger and going into dangerous neighborhoods when we have no compelling reason to be there. With guns carried for personal protection, we balance the danger of not possessing a means of decisive personal defense against the inherent danger of handing loaded gun. Through the scrupulous practice of gun safety, we render safe the inherently dangerous activity of handing a gun every day. For the concealed carry practitioner, who will regularly handle a loaded gun, this entails three separate principles–

#1 Never point a gun at anything you are not willing to shoot, injure, kill or destroy.

#2 Keep your finger off the trigger and well outside the trigger guard until you have decided to shoot and the gun is pointed at whatever you intend to shoot.

#3 Be sure you are legally entitled to shoot what- or whomever you have decided to shoot, that you can take the shot with safety to yourself and any innocent who may be forward and beyond the muzzle.

Concern #1 emphasizes a safety provision I've really harped on in this chapter. Before handling a gun, you must select a safe direction into which you will point it. Out in public, inside your car in a public parking lot, in a public restroom, or in the private restroom at your office or in your home, in a multi-story condominium, and many, many other places, there simply is no safe direction beyond which, if you negligently discharge your gun, no one may be in the path of the bullet, as it tears through drywall and other common construction materials. Think your car door will stop a bullet? Think again.

Concern #2 is a training issue. As we discussed in the *Beginning Training* chapter, you must develop an unbreakable habit of indexing your finger off the trigger and up on the frame of the gun, well away from the trigger guard, any time the gun is in your hand but it is not raised to point at the target that you have decided to shoot. The same, of course, applies to the actual use of a firearm to defend against a violent human assailant. When the gun is coming out of the holster, before it is pointed at the assailant and you have decided you have no recourse but to shoot him or her, your finger must not come near the trigger. Negligently shooting an innocent bystander before your gun is trained on the assailant is indefensible and you will have to answer for any bullets you fire.

A more common danger, though, is discharging a gun during casual gun handling. There is a hint in that sentence! Gun handling should never be casual. Gun handling must always be done with your complete attention on the gun and on handling it safely. If you are not able to give two seconds of your undivided attention to moving your gun, do not handle your gun. If there is no safe, bullet-stopping backstop into which you can point your gun, do not handle it. If you are in a physical condition in which you cannot practice scrupulous gun safety–if you are extremely stressed, physically or mentally exhausted, impaired by any drug, substance (prescription or other) or by alcohol–do not, please do not, handle a gun. Leave it in its holster, leave it in its lock box or gun safe, but do not handle it until you have the clarity of mind to concentrate entirely on gun safety.

---

(1) www.corneredcat.com, an extensive website written by Kathy Jackson, supplemented by her extensive book, "Cornered Cat: A Woman's Guide to Concealed Carry, published by White Feather Press, www.whitefeatherpress.com, 269-838-5586.

(2) Shot Lock, http://www.shotlock.com, 800-967-8107, ShotLock, a division of TruckVault Inc., P. O. Box 734 Sedro Woolley WA 98284

(3) VLine Industries, 370 Easy St., Simi Valley, CA 93065. 805-520-4987 http://www.vlineind.com

CARRYING YOUR HANDGUN

Before carrying your holstered gun in public, you need complete confidence that it will remain concealed. Worry about concealment influences how you move, how you stand and what you do with your hands. If the holster shifts forward, back or away from your body, it is more prone to show and it will attract your concern. You'll surreptitiously try to move the gun and holster back where it belongs. If you are in public, it is pretty clear to onlookers what you are doing. By resolving concealment and holster movement, we go far to eliminate physical "tells" that others will recognize as indicating you've got a gun.

Armed citizens new to concealed carry complain that they feel terribly self-conscious when wearing a gun in public. That's natural, since any big change in clothing or accessories awakens our internal critic. Do you remember your first pair of really high heels? The ones with the four- or five-inch spike heels? You had to be pretty careful as you walked the first few times you wore them, didn't you? If you wore that kind of shoe with any regularity, it got a lot easier, didn't it? The same is true for concealed carry.

Probably the easiest way to get through the uncomfortable early stages of concealed carry is to carry your holstered handgun for as many of your waking hours as possible, starting out at home. I can already hear readers' dismayed cries, "Why would I carry a gun at home? That's where I lock the doors so I can relax and run around in my pajamas!" Before rejecting my suggestion out of hand, think about this: Only through repetition do we become comfortable with and proficient at any new practice. Carrying a holstered handgun is a new experience. Only through many hours of carrying your gun under a variety of circumstances–standing, sitting, reclining, walking, during vigorous or hurried activity, and while at leisure–can you expect to become fully comfortable with the practice of carrying a self-defense gun on your body.

Before getting into the details of handgun concealment, we should resolve bigger mistakes that reveal to others that you are carrying a handgun. What is the biggest threat to failing to conceal your handgun? You are! If you are uneasy about carrying a concealed handgun, the frequent adjustments to your holster— the tugs to be sure your clothing is covering the gun, the little touches you make to be sure everything is still in place—are all "tells" that loudly announce, "I'm carrying a gun, and I'm pretty worried about it!"

We make these little adjustments either when the gun and holster move around or when we are uncertain that our clothing is concealing all the gear well enough, as may happen with a shirt or vest that is just an inch or two too short. In later pages, we will list high-quality holsters and accessories that will keep the gun from moving around, and that is an important element. Inevitably, though, shirts will ride up and waistbands shift a little when you sit down or stand up. Especially when new to carrying concealed, giving a little tug to the waistband and

Don't do this! Adjusting a holstered gun through a cover shirt is still obviously adjusting a holstered gun.

pulling down on the shirt to be sure the gun is still covered is almost irresistible. If you must adjust clothing, just exercise caution to do it where no one can see. For example, do those tugs and repositionings before getting out of your car, after a quick check around to be sure no one is watching.

While it is easy to advise you to put on the gun and holster and then leave it alone, practicing that advice is pretty challenging if the holster and magazine or speed loader pouches move around on the belt. Prevention is primarily found in using a high-quality holster and pouches made specifically for the brand and model of your handgun. Then, carry them on a high-quality gun belt that positions them stably in one position. When possible, buy all three from the same leatherworker. Make a few adjustments to your wardrobe to assure a selection of clothing that is a little longer and fuller to cover the gear.

When getting started carrying concealed or breaking in new gear, wear it for several days at home in complete privacy, where problems will become apparent and can be resolved without worrying that someone will glimpse you adjusting your gun. In breaking in a new holster over a recent weekend, I found that I had to take extra care to hook the belt clips all the way over the lower edge of my belt. After I became aware of the issue and took greater care when putting on the rig, the gun and holster have not ridden up as if they were getting ready to jump out of my waistband and make a run for it. Had I started wearing the holster in public the first day, I could have faced a real challenge finding a place private enough to get the holster tucked back inside the waistband and hooked back onto the belt. As it was, the learning episode was no big deal.

With a new gun or a new holster, take the time over a weekend or in the evenings to discover, through trial and error, which combinations of trousers, belts and holsters provide the most stable carry platform for your concealed handgun. The home-test should also reveal if the position in which you are wearing the holstered gun is subject to catching on chair arms, banging into doorways, or otherwise clearly communicating that you have a foreign metallic object strapped to your person that, really, can only be a gun.

When you are carrying a concealed handgun on a belt holster, there are certain ranges of movement you must learn to avoid. At home, stand in front of

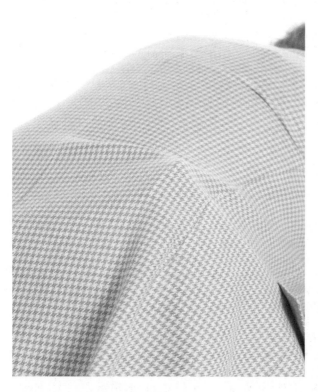

a full length mirror and practice squatting down instead of leaning over by bending at the waist, as may be necessary to get an item off a bottom shelf in the supermarket or the stockroom at work, for example. Depending on where you position your holster, you'll find a good way to execute a normal range of motion without letting the grips of the gun make a recognizable outline through the fabric of your covering garment.

Once you have proven your carry system at home, you will enjoy the benefits of confidence in the concealability of your handgun and the holster, belt and related accessories. Proven concealment greatly alleviates the urge

Belt-holstered handguns will "print" when you bend over, reach down or lean forward in your chair.

to make adjustments or to touch the gear to be sure it is hidden.

Before carrying your gun in a new holster, check to be sure there is no danger of your gun falling out of the holster. Unload your gun, triple-check to be sure it is unloaded, then put it in the holster and tip it upside down and at various angles to see if the gun moves. Poor retention is a serious defect. If the gun falls out easily, return the holster or carry device to the store or manufacturer. One of the holster's main jobs is to retain the gun securely until you need to draw it.

Some holsters, even a few very high-end ones, have a waxy polish or finish that can squeak as the holster's loops rub against the belt. Resolve this problem during that in-home test period before wearing a squeaky belt and holster in public!

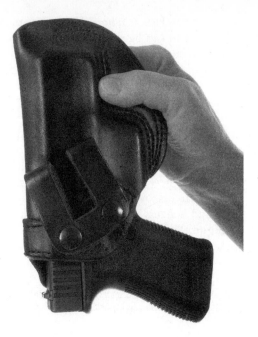

Testing a holster for retention by turning it upside down. Kramer IWB passes with flying colors.

BEST CONCEALMENT POSITIONS

There is no single best concealment position that I could recommend for you, since variations from one woman to the next include petite, regular and tall torso lengths and differences in curviness that increase the hip angle when the hip measurement is considerably greater than the waistline. What are some of the more popular gun carry positions and how do they work for different figures?

Envision your waistline and the positions around it on which you might carry a handgun. Borrowing from an analog clock, your belt buckle sits at 12 o'clock, and the small of your back is 6 o'clock; your right hip is 3 o'clock, and your left is 9. The 3 and 9 o'clock positions are the most exposed, and a gun carried out on that point will be not only be quite uncomfortable, but vulnerable to banging into doorways, catching on chair arms, and just plain sticking out where nothing short of an oversized raincoat will conceal it.

Some people feel that their gun is concealed with the handgun holstered at 6 o'clock, called small of the back, or SOB, carry, but that only lasts as long as you stand with your back perfectly straight. When you assume any posture except standing perfectly erect, the hollow created by the small of the back disappears, and the grips of the guns will catch on your shirt and pull it up, or pro-

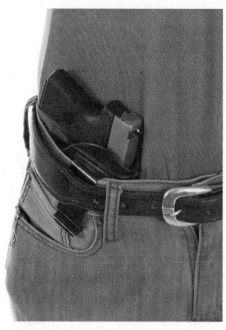

Even a small gun and holster worn right on point of hip is uncomfortable and creates a lumpy protrusion that really shows beyond the line of the body, as the hip bone pushes it out, decreasing concealability. Move the same gun and holster forward to appendix carry (ABOVE) or just behind the point of the hip (LEFT) to improve concealability. Away from the hard bone of the hip, the gun and holster can sink into and better blend with the torso.

trude to make an outline beneath your concealing clothing that can really be nothing except the grips of a handgun.

The unmistakable outline of the pistol grips beneath covering clothing is called "printing." It occurs any time the grips protrude more than an inch or two beyond your waistline unless covered by a bulky or fluffy garment, like a down-filled vest.

A lot of variables determine how well your gun and holster are concealed. These include the shape of your body, the holster in which you carry your gun, the angle at which the rig positions the gun, the size of your carry gun and your general style of clothing. With practice, you will find a place on your figure that is least susceptible to printing a holstered gun. For women with a less curvy "boyish" figure, this spot may be immediately behind the strong-side hip; for ladies with a very curvy hourglass figure, it may be just forward of the strong-side hip or in cross draw position just in front of the weak-side hip. A short-barreled gun carried at an angle right behind the strong-side hip conveniently allows you to conceal the gun with even open-fronted jackets and vests.

SOB holster lets pistol grips get caught on clothing.

For some, a shoulder holster may be the answer, and we'll study this carry method more in detail in a later chapter. A shoulder holster may conceal well if you are full-figured through the torso, because the upper body must be thick enough to camouflage the bulk of the gun, whether that is the grips of a gun holstered muzzle down, or the length of the slide of one carried in the more common grips-down orientation, with the muzzle horizontal and pointing toward the rear. If your torso is thinner than the length of the holster or the length of the gun from muzzle to backstrap, the outline of the muzzle will show through clothing out the back. A vertical carry shoulder holster solves this somewhat, though on a thin person the grips will print along your left breast if you are right handed, and the torso appears wider on the gun side unless the jacket or bolero you conceal beneath is rather loose or bulky with a gathered or boxy profile.

Others may recommend ankle holsters for concealment, but the restrictions on wardrobe for this carry method are even more onerous, and drawing from an ankle holster while running toward safety is nearly impossible. Still, because this is one of the common holster alternatives, we'll discuss ankle holsters in a later chapter, too, because this concealment method does have particular

functionality for armed citizens in certain situations.

It seems that every day some creative entrepreneur is introducing a non-holster or quasi-holster concealed carry alternative. Some are functional, but others apparently look better on paper than they actually work on the human body. Rarely do the non-holster alternatives provide a single carry method that works seven days a week, day in and day out. Still, we'll look at these carry methods, but first, let's learn about more time-proven concealed carry holsters.

Bulges from shoulder holsters happen when the muzzle pokes out the back.

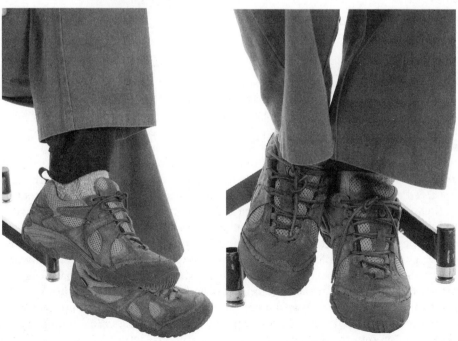

Ankle holsters may be revealed if you sit down wrong, as we see with legs crossed at the knee (LEFT). It works better if you sit with your ankles together, tucked under the chair. (RIGHT)

14

BELTS ARE THE MAGIC FOUNDATION

Have you ever driven past a mobile home park after a tornado or hurricane wiped out the trailers and wondered how all those poor people expected to survive the disaster in homes that literally had no foundations? Carrying a handgun and holster on a thin, floppy belt is about the same kind of mistake! If your belt is thin, soft or floppy, you've tried to build a concealed carry system without the proper foundation, and failure awaits.

A handgun in a holster weighs anywhere from one to three pounds. That is enough weight and bulk that, if the belt to which the holster is connected is too narrow or too thin, or if it is soft and flexible, the holster and gun will flop fore and aft and outboard, away from the body. For belts, thickness from two dimensions is important. Not only is a reasonable density necessary to provide a somewhat rigid platform, but the belt needs to be at least one inch wide if not $1\frac{1}{4}$ inches wide from top to bottom. With all the commercial emphasis on the gun and the holster, too many people fail to understand that the belt to which the holstered gun is attached does most of the work in stabilizing the carry system.

One value of training and practice is the habituated snap the hand makes right on to the grips of the gun without having to stop and think about exactly where the gun is located. If the holster and gun move around on the belt, all that practice and training is for naught. If it is not always in the same place, you will have to find your gun before you can draw and use it. The tenth or quarter of a second needed to catch up to or get ahead of the assailant's attack might just be gained by being able to put your hand immediately on the grips of your gun and moving into the next phase of your response, be that issuing verbal orders or drawing to present the firearm.

WHAT IS A GUN BELT?

The term "gun belt" conjures visions of a wide, heavy equipment belt like those worn by law enforcement officers. This is not what is required for successful concealed carry in a belt holster. There are a number of comfortable belt options from which to choose that are made in various colors and contours. You can even add a custom buckle to dress it up if you prefer.

Lisa Looper, inventor of the celebrated women's Flashbang holster, also sells women's gun belts but makes them of such nicely finished, stylish materials that, especially with today's lower waistlines, they make a nice alternative for women with a more athletic build and less accentuated hip-to-waist curve.

If you find wearing a belt generally uncomfortable, or if the edges of the belt cut into your hip or stomach, try wearing a contour cut belt. Instead of the flat strip of stiffened leather from which belts are usually made, a contoured belt is cut on a curve so that the bottom of the belt is a little wider than the top to match the flare of the hip. Ladies aren't straight up and down and our belts shouldn't be either. You'll find contoured gun belts from manufacturers like Galco,[2] Comp-Tac,[3] Milt Sparks,[4] Bianchi,[5] Ted Blocker[6] and Wild Bill's,[7] to identify only a few who include contour belts in their regular product catalog.

In addition to the contour, a tapered belt reduces pressure against the stomach, and for ladies in particular, this can really make a difference in comfort. The taper reduces the width of the front of the belt and works best if you are carrying at or behind the hip. It also serves to

Up and coming women's holster maker Lisa Looper (famous for the Flashbang holster which we'll discuss later) recently introduced a line of very attractive gun belts that come with stylish buckles, great textures and finishes, a thin Kydex® insert to add durable rigidity, and even gorgeous brilliantly-colored suede backings.[1]

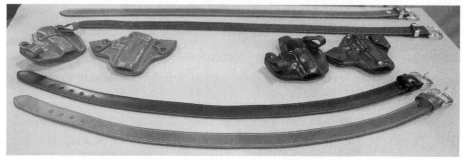

Aker International [8] holsters hand cut the contour belts they sell.

Various contoured belts show the available variety. From top to bottom, Galco International, 5 Shot Leather,[9] Bianchi,[10] Mitch Rosen Extraordinary Gun Leather,[11] 5 Shot Leather, and the bottom two also by Galco International. This display lets you see the variations – some leather workers put in only the slightest of curves, while others use a substantial curve, which will be more comfortable for ladies with a very angled hipline.

reduce the masculine appearance of wearing a thick, heavy belt, so a front taper is useful in maintaining a feminine appearance, too.

Conversely, Tom Kulwicki of Alessi Holsters [12] does not believe that cutting the curve of the contour into the belt is a good idea. To help you make an educated decision, let's consider his opinion, too. Cutting a curved belt does not allow the natural grain of the leather to keep its rigidity, and the belt that is cut off the natural grain of the leather will break down earlier, he explains. Instead, he recommends, buy one high-quality gun belt and let the leather naturally contour to the wearer's curves over the years. Kulwicki shows his own belt, which he has worn for some twenty years, pointing out how it has achieved its own rounded contour. He recommends that the double-layer leather construction, with his special skiving to add rigidity, is a better long term solution.

By the time we've specified a contoured and tapered gun belt, it is entirely possible that the belt you really need for concealed carry comfort is too specialized to be stocked at your local gun store, and possibly not even made by the big holster companies. Galco makes a contoured and tapered belt; Mitch

A one-inch wide, tapered dress belt Mitch Rosen made for the author many years ago, worn with his ultra-concealable American Rear Guard holster.

Rosen makes a tapered belt but does not stock a contour cut in his product line. Likewise, Alessi Holsters sells a nice tapered belt, though it will start life as a straight, non-contoured belt. Because high-quality gun belts are expensive, it makes sense to go the extra mile to get what works for you.

Acquiring a contoured and tapered gun belt may require finding and working with a smaller business where a leatherworker can hand-make a belt with the details you want and need. My daily carry belt, holster and magazine pouch set comes from John Ralston of 5 Shot Leather,[9] who has been very kind in the face of my rather specific belt and holster needs. Use word of mouth, Internet research and intel from gun magazines to compile a list of reputable holster makers, and then contact them with your specifications to find someone who will make exactly what you need and want. The expense of buying a single, custom concealed carry system, purchased once and worn for years, is far less than the trial-and-error method of buying a dozen different holsters, three or four belts, and probably a different gun or two as you try to find something that works for you.

Beyond the curve and taper of the belt, a successful concealed carry belt needs a certain amount of stiffness so that the weight of the gun doesn't pull it away from your torso. This is particularly true if you carry in a belt scabbard outside the waistband, where the fabric of the trousers can't help to hold the gun in place.

There are several ways to stiffen a belt made of leather. Two-layer belts carry weight a lot better than a single layer of soft leather, even when the single layer alone is thicker than a leatherworker's skillful combination of two thinner layers. In addition, different cuts of leather have different degrees of pliability. An inexpensive belt may be made out of soft, flexible sections of the hide, and while these sell affordably as fashion accents, they are entirely worthless for concealed carry.

A professional holster maker who sells belts and holsters of flawless quality is unlikely to accept second-rate materials, and may well demand the shoulder portion of the cowhide, so that the belt is naturally stiffer. Other holster and gun belt makers work in horsehide, which by nature tends toward more stiffness in thinner pieces. Finally, some leatherworkers increase stiffness by using a particular stitching pattern sewn through two layers; others apply proprietary solutions to stiffen the leather, or insert very thin sheets of rigid plastic between the front and back layer for a belt that will remain stiff through years of wear. There are

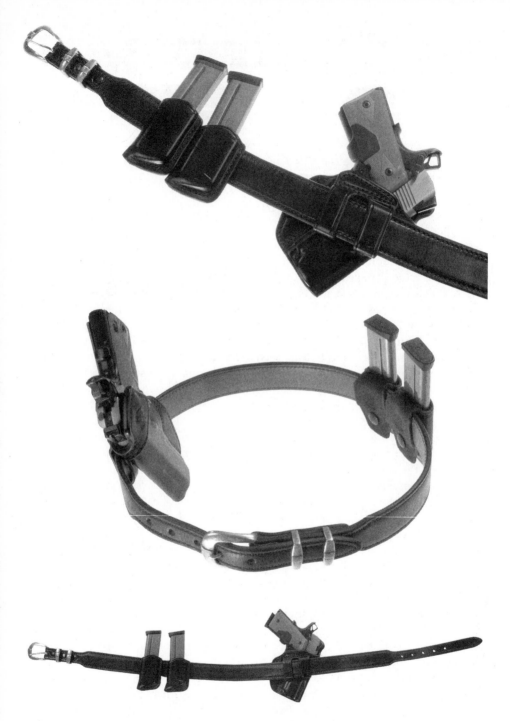

John Ralston created this 5 Shot Leather contour cut and tapered belt, holster and magazine pouch set in black leather. The author added a custom silver buckle and belt keepers.

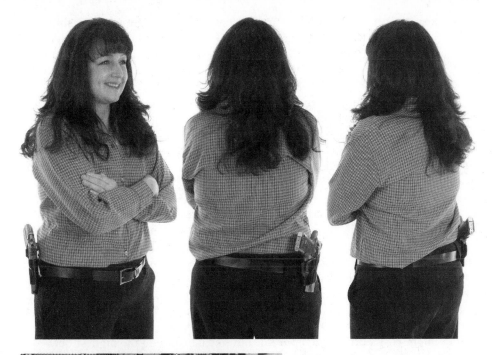

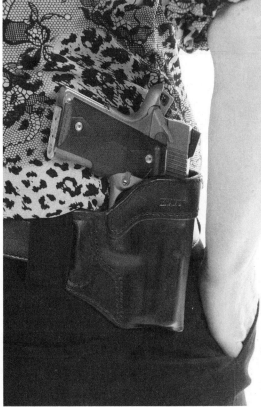

ABOVE: *The gun butt, weighed down by a magazine full of ammunition, flops away from the body on a flimsy belt. By comparison, notice how this expertly-designed Kramer Handgun Leather Vertical Scabbard tucks in tight against body when worn on a sturdy belt* (LEFT).

quite a few ways to increase belt stiffness, so keep that in mind when you are buying concealed carry gear. You do not need to settle for a substandard belt that is soft and floppy or overcompensate with a belt that is about ¼-inch thick and still won't work well.

In addition, some armed citizens prefer nylon gun belts. You may find a leather belt preferable because it can be contoured and tapered, looks a little dressier and is less likely to draw unwanted attention. The width of the belt is another aspect that can make a gun belt look oddly masculine or unfashionable. Most holsters have belt loops that fit a 1 1/4-inch belt, though some go up to 1 1/2 inch or wider. Thicker belt loops usually become a special order item, and a wider belt is usually a little more uncomfortable around your mid-section, so few ladies favor the wider options.

A few gun belt makers and custom holster makers can make sufficiently rigid one-inch dress gun belts favored by many, though you will find it considerably more challenging to find a holster with one-inch belt slots or loops. Why not just string the one-inch belt through a holster's 1 1/4- or 1 1/2-inch loop? The answer is instability. The holster will move up and down and, particularly when you draw the gun, you will have to overcome that extra movement. For best results, holster and belt loops need to be custom-fit to eliminate movement.

I am a big proponent of buying concealed carry gear as a set. The belt, holster and magazine or speed loader pouches need to come from the same leatherworker or holster manufacturer. That way they can fit the width and thickness of the belt to work smoothly with the holster's belt slots or loops. Because of the different ways that gun belts are constructed, thickness varies a lot, and you may find it very difficult to pull the belt through the belt slots if a different holster maker made the holster with the expectation that it would be used on a slightly thinner belt. Buying sets from one manufacturer or custom holster maker might cost a little more up front, but like demanding the highest quality you can afford for any big-budget purchase, it saves money and hassle in the long run.

---

(1) Flashbang Holsters, 2124 S. Prospect, Oklahoma City, OK 73120, 405-677-1655, http://flashbang-holsters.publishpath.com/holster-belts

(2) Galco International, 2019 West Quail Avenue, Phoenix, AZ 85027, 800-874-2526 www.usgalco.com

(3) Comp-Tac Victory Gear, P.O. Box 1809, Spring, Texas 77383-1809, 866-441-9157 http://www.comp-tac.com/product_info.php?products_id=43&osCsid=5mstgoil8f8n39peom5re3rtp6)

(4) Milt Sparks Holsters Inc., 115 E. 44th St., Boise, ID 83714, 208-377-5577 www.miltsparks.com/Belts.htm

(5) Bianchi International, a division of Safariland, 3120 E. Mission Blvd. Ontario, CA 91761 800-347-1200, http://www.bianchi-intl.com/product/CatList.php?numSubCat=30

(6) Ted Blocker Holsters, 9438 SW Tigard St., Tigard, OR 97223, 503-670-7972 http://www.tedblocker-holsters.com/product.cfm?pi=7C78E5D3-9DC6-3E9A-8827C9CAD9AA8ED7

(7) Wild Bill's Concealment, 2664 Timber Drive, #341, Garner, NC 27529, 919-779-9582 http://www.wildbillsconcealment.com

(8) Alessi Holsters, 247 Cayuga North, Cheektowaga, NY 14225, 716-932-7497, http://www.alessigun-holsters.com

(8) Aker International, Inc., 2248 Main Street, Suite 6, Chula Vista, California 91911-3932, 619-423-5182, http://akerleather.com

(9) 5 Shot Leather, LLC, 18018 N Lidgerwood Ct., Colbert, WA 99005, 509-844-3969, http://www.5shotleather.com/index.htm

(10) Bianchi International, a division of Safariland, 13386 International Parkway, Jacksonville, FL 32218, 800-347-1200, http://www.bianchi-intl.com/

(11) Mitch Rosen Extraordinary Gunleather, LLC, 540 No. Commercial Street, Manchester, New Hampshire 03101-1122, 603-647-2971, http://www.mitchrosen.com

THE BASIC
BELT HOLSTER

If you tried to wear your husband's blue jeans, would you conclude that you couldn't wear trousers because the borrowed pair was too long and too loose, and you fell down when you tripped on the dragging hems? Well, why should borrowing someone else's holster be any different? Too often we defeat ourselves before we ever get started. "I tried to carry a gun in an old holster my husband let me use. It was really uncomfortable. I guess I just can't carry a gun in a belt holster!" Yes, that is a common complaint when women attend defensive handgun classes where working out of a belt holster is part of the curriculum.

To introduce the topic of holsters, we must start with the most common type, the belt holster. An almost endless variety of belt holsters exists. While all the options seem baffling when you are getting started, after trying a dozen that only kind of work for your figure, your gun and your style of dress, you quickly realize all those options are important as you refine your holster needs and wants.

Before discussing any more details, we need to identify the common types of belt holsters, categorized by the locations in which they are worn. Holsters attached to a belt and worn inside the waistband are called IWBs, and those worn on a belt outside the fabric of the trousers are called OWBs, shorthand for outside [the] waistband. Where the holster is worn is also reflected in the name game, with "strong side" self-explanatory as is small of back carry, often abbreviated as SOB. A cross-draw holster is worn forward of the weak-side hip with the grips toward the belly button; a holster designed for appendix carry is positioned forward of the strong-side hip, with the grips oriented toward the hip. There are all sorts of variations, and in this chapter we will introduce the most prominent.

Traditionally, holsters, like belts, were made of leather, which lends itself to molding to match the gun's contours. Kydex®, a thermoplastic with a high-temperature melting point, has the same moldability with noteworthy durability, and often is sold at a lower price point since the molding is done thermally, instead of accomplished by hand tooling. Both materials have positive and negative characteristics. Kydex® can wear off a gun's finish, but won't retain moisture so is unlikely to encourage rust. Leather can be quieter when the gun is drawn, though I question if we overestimate our ability to move in utter silence through dangerous areas, so this point may be moot.

Kydex® generally releases the gun more easily then leather, and its prominence in competitive shooting like IDPA[3] and IPSC[4] is surely a testament to the speed advantages of the Kydex® material used for holsters.

Some holster makers like FIST, Inc.[5] ingeniously laminate a thin layer of Kydex® inside an outer layer of leather. The holster is indestructibly rigid, fast from which to draw, but has the beauty of leather.

While some holsters can be carried in several positions, most are designed to fit and conceal best in one specific position. I don't have a lot of faith in one-size-fits-all designs, and the same applies to holsters made for use in several locations. For best results, find one expertly-crafted holster and use it the way its designer intended. Common carry positions are on the strong side right behind the hip, in front of the strong-side hip called appendix carry, and just forward of the weak-side hip called cross draw. We already

Belt holsters can be worn in a variety of locations around the waist, including strong side forward of the hip (TOP), strong side immediately behind the hip (LEFT) and cross draw (ABOVE).

discussed small of the back carry.

The most common concealed carry position is at or immediately behind the strong side hip. When the holster is substantially angled, many women achieve a reasonable degree of holster comfort in this position, especially with an OWB holster design.

Forward of the strong side hip is called appendix carry. What this position gives up in concealment it pays back in comfort for women who have a noticeable curve at the hip.

Belt holsters are designed to sit at various angles, called cant or rake. A neutral rake positions the barrel of the gun perpendicular to the beltline, in other words, entirely vertical. The most common rake angles the muzzle about 15 degrees to the rear, though there are holsters designed with less or more angle—sometimes a little, sometimes a lot. In addition, a few holsters angle the muzzle of the pistol forward, and this is a particularly effective method to carry a short-barreled handgun holstered just forward of the hip, since the angle alleviates the uncomfortable pressure of the barrel pressing down into the iliac crest of the hipbone. Mitch Rosen's Nancy Special[1] or Galco's Stinger,[2] both OWB holsters, exemplify the forward cant design, though there are others mounted on adjustable hardware that could be rotated to this angle, too.

A few holsters, mostly an artifact of times past, positioned the barrel of the gun nearly horizontal, usually carried at or near the small of the back, with the grips poking up where the strong-side hand could snake around to draw the gun. Now only a few holster makers sell small of the back holsters, and it is usually positioned at about a 45-degree rake. Small of the back carry is rarely truly concealable, as discussed earlier. In addition, should you be knocked to the ground in the process of an attack, access to a small of the back holster nearly impossible without rolling over, and the assailant may block you from doing so. If you fall, there exists real potential for spinal injury from some part of the gun crushing nerves, disks and vertebra. Avoid this carry position; there are others that conceal far better and aren't so risky.

In addition to carry position and angle, other defining features among various holster designs are how high the holster sits on the belt and how the rig attaches to the belt. Some OWB holsters have a belt loop that is a little leather tunnel sewn on the back of the holster. Such a substantial attachment point lends the holster considerable stability on the belt. Alternatively, the material from which the holster is made may extend beyond the sides of an OWB holster, and belt slots may be cut into these. The location of the belt loops or other attachment determines how the holster is positioned on the belt. A high-ride holster's belt loops attach near the bottom of the holster, mid-rise attaches somewhere around the center, and a holster designed to sit low on the belt has belt loops right at the mouth of the holster.

Some holster designers have attempted to make extended loops to drop the holster below the waistline, because women usually have best success with a holster that sits as low on the belt as possible. Sometimes the belt loop attachment will extend above the mouth of the holster on a shank or elongated belt loop assembly to lower the holster even more. The more extreme variations of

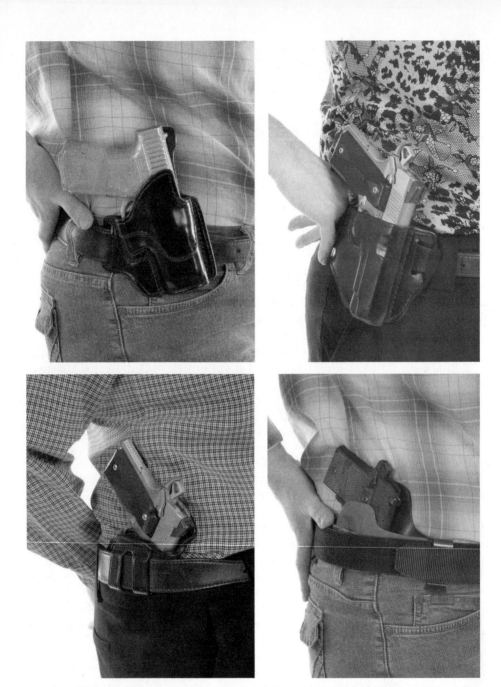

A variety of holsters illustrate the angles different designs use to increase holster comfort, including the muzzle forward cant of a Don Hume holster worn muzzle forward of the strong side hip (TOP LEFT). Haugen Handgun Leather's Huntington Wedge is a neutral rake OWB demonstrated here just forward of the hip. Worn just behind the hip, (TOP RIGHT) John Ralston's 5 Shot Leather IWB (BOTTOM LEFT), and Devin Wulle's White Dog IWB (BOTTOM RIGHT), combining a Kydex® holster attached to a wide leather backing for comfort and concealability.

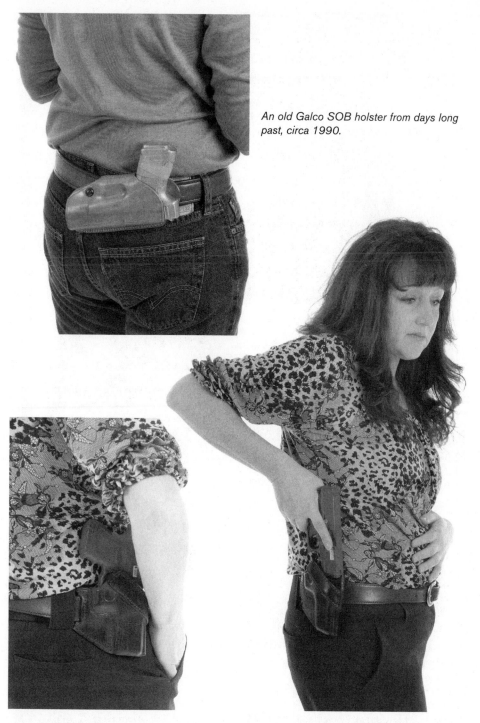

An old Galco SOB holster from days long past, circa 1990.

High ride holsters, like this one by Rusty Sherrick, can use an angled speed cut to ease drawing and holstering.

Blade Tech Dropped and Offset holster for carry and shown in action (TOP). Drawing from Kramer's Women's Scabbard (BOTTOM) requires very little elbow lift, but concealing gun in it requires long, loose clothing.

this OWB design are known as dropped and offset holsters, and while they are very fast from which to draw, they are not very concealable. Their primary use is in competitive shooting, where both shooters of both genders appreciate the way more room between the gun grips and their torso speeds drawing. An early proponent of a dropped holster design for women was Kramer Leather, which still makes their Women's Belt Scabbard. For a time, Galco also produced one of the first women's dropped and offset holsters, a simple leather scabbard attached to a wide plastic shank, though it is no longer in sold. Today, the primary source for dropped and offset competition holsters is Comp-Tac [6] and Blade-Tech Industries[7], though Kramer Leather [8] and Ted Blocker Holsters [9] market dropped and offset OWB holsters, as do others.

Women, many of whom are short-waisted, benefit from dropped and offset holsters because carrying the gun lower on the torso moves the grips of the gun out and away from the ribcage and positions the barrel of the gun below the hipbone. Both the ribcage and the hip's wide crest are areas of considerable holster

discomfort. In addition, lowering the holster alleviates the struggle to draw, which is difficult when you have trouble raising the muzzle above the mouth of the holster. Owing to women's generally shorter torsos, this is a bigger problem for female shooters than it is for men. Ask a man of average build to stand next to a woman of identical height, and in most cases the man's torso will be longer than the woman's; more of her height comes from her legs. This general characteristic is exaggerated with the petite, short-waisted figure.

Though Chris Cunningham is shorter than her husband Grant, this photo shows that their legs are essentially the same length, as emphasized by the height of both belts. Because Chris' torso is so much shorter, the grips of the Glock Model 26 poke painfully into her rib cage, and drawing requires her to lift her elbow above shoulder level. Both are shown wearing identical pistols and identical Kramer belt scabbards, from which Grant enjoys a reasonable draw stroke because so much of his height is in the length of his torso.

When a short-waisted woman draws from a mid- or high-ride holster, the lift required to clear leather (a colloquialism meaning to draw the muzzle above the mouth of the holster) will typically entail lifting her elbow above shoulder height. On the range, you'll see all kinds of funny contortions like dropping the hip forward, twisting the torso or elaborately bending the wrist to achieve enough lift to yank the gun out of the holster. Unfortunately, all these contortions are slower than a straight lift out of the holster, as may be accomplished if the rig fits perfectly on the shooter's body. In response, the industry brought us the "dropped" element in the dropped and offset holster.

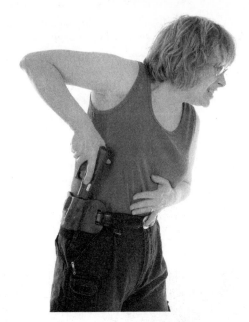

While few holsters will be as comfortable as a dropped and offset design, the comfort comes at a price. First, concealment is severely compromised, by both riding low on the hip and by extending the grips a couple of inches beyond the hip. Next, attaching the holster to an elongated shank creates a fulcrum, increasing odds that the holster will move up with the gun during the draw, described as "following." When this happens, the holster feels as though it is stuck on the gun. This is not true of all the dropped and offset rigs, but is a drawback of which to be aware.

Canting the holster severely on the belt, orienting the muzzle either to the front or to the back, eases the drawing problems the dropped and offset design tries to alleviate, but without its inherent lack of concealment as the gun and holster are allowed to snug in close to the body. Drawing a gun from a deeply

A woman drawing from a standard belt holster has a very hard time getting the gun muzzle above the holster mouth. Getting the gun out of the holster is much easier when the same woman draws from a dropped and offset holster, which is easy to use but nearly impossible to conceal.

Holster angle helps avoid jabbing the gun's grips into the ribcage and hip bone. John Ralston's 5-Shot Leather IWB (LEFT) and Mitch Rosen's Nancy Special (RIGHT) holsters are great examples of this holster comfort principle at work.

angled holster does require some degree of wrist flexibility, as well as top quality holster design for good retention. Still, a canted holster goes a long way toward increasing ease of draw, wearing comfort and concealability. A high-end example of this holster design is Mitch Rosen's American Rear Guard.

Another feature that eases the short-torsoed shooter's difficulties in drawing from a standard holster is the "speed cut," a feature also borrowed from competitive shooting, that cuts away part of the front of the holster. Done right, even a moderate speed cut helps, though it requires skillful design so the holster maintains good retention qualities.

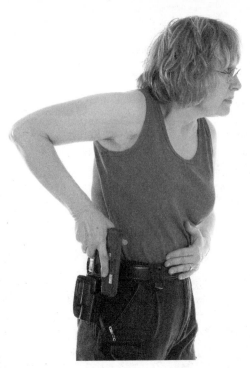

Holster height becomes even more critical with trousers worn higher on the waist, as we see with these Royal Robbins' hiking pants. Blade Tech holster with speed cut, viewed from the front at the point in the draw stroke at which the gun comes free of the holster. (ABOVE) While Rusty Sherrick's Gochenour Extreme High Ride holster sits a lot higher on the belt, its speed cut also eases drawing contortions. (LEFT AND BELOW)

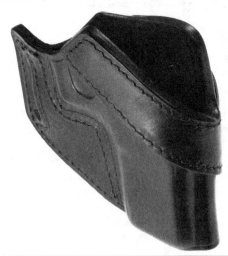

OWB HOLSTERS

Speed cuts are effective on holsters worn on a belt outside of the clothing. Belt holsters come in several varieties, and the outside the waistband (OWB) scabbards that we've been discussing are the most common. These attach to the belt and hang down outside the trousers, where drawing access is unparalleled. Concealing a gun holstered outside the waistband requires a concealment shirt, jacket or vest of slightly fuller cut, and one that is long enough to cover an inch or two below the bottom of the holster so it is not exposed during normal range of movement.

An OWB belt scabbard is comfortable when guns are carried openly, as is done at training classes, competitive pistol shooting events, at home, on the farm, or when practicing open carry. The latter practice does require a higher level of gun retention than many of the open-topped holsters provide, be that a retention strap across the top (called a thumb break for how it is disengaged), or a lock on the trigger guard released by means of a button or lever. Other belt holsters are designed to tuck the holstered gun tight against the body. With these, you can enjoy surprising concealability when wearing a longer jacket, vest or tunic.

Tightly tucking a holster against the body is usually accomplished by the design of the holster's belt loops or slots. On OWB scabbards, one successful method has been attaching a broad tunnel loop to the back of the holster through which the belt slides, then adding a tab at the rear of the holster through which a belt slot is cut. The loop on the extended tab helps pull in the entire holster against the body. You will also see holsters made with a noticeable concavity to snug the holster against the body contour, as exemplified by Mitch Rosen's line of OWB holsters and the Galco Concealable.

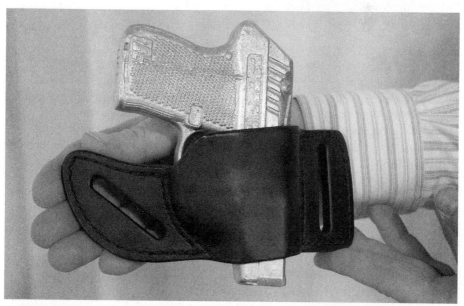

The "wings" on Lisa Looper's "Sophia" holster help pull the rig in close to the body.

The wings principle is at work in this Alessi CQC-S holster, as well.

Some holsters are attached to a broad concave paddle that is slipped inside the clothing while the gun hangs on the outside. The paddle, made of plastic or leather, distributes the weight of the gun, so some find paddle holsters more comfortable. Some promote the paddle holster for use without a belt, but I would not recommend it. The weight of the gun and holster pull on the fabric waistband, letting the gun flop away from the body where its outline can be identified through covering garments. Unless secured to a belt, the gun and holster may move so much that they are not always in the same place when you need to draw. Without the support of a belt, both the paddle holster and the holstered gun can come out when the shooter draws. In recent years, I've seen the addition of some very aggressive teeth on paddles to keep the holster attached to the clothing during the draw stroke, though the long-term effect on the fabric of a waistband could be destructive.

The creative men and women building concealed carry gear have other tricks up their sleeves that encourage holsters to hug the body for better concealability, too, with new ways being regularly pioneered. If you are shopping

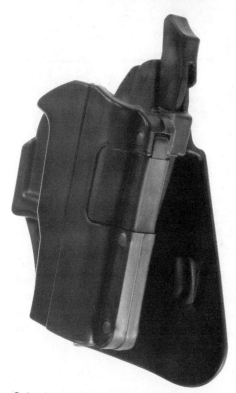

Take a look at the backs of Greg Kramer's Speed Scabbard (UPPER LEFT) and this older Alessi IWB (LEFT), holsters that use a substantial belt loop tunnel to stabilize the holster on the belt. Along the same lines, the Rusty Sherrick holster (ABOVE) uses a stabilizing tunnel belt loop plus an extended loop at the rear of the holster to hold the gun tight against the body.

Galco International paddle holster.

online, don't buy unless the holster is photographed on a real person, and there are enough pictures from various angles showing you how much it protrudes away from the body during carry. Also be aware that the varying curves of the individual figure will push parts of the holster in or out, so that what conceals well on one figure may not do so well on another.

IWB HOLSTERS

The inside the waistband (IWB) holster offers a higher level of concealability, using the waistband of your trousers to not only tuck the holstered gun in tight against your body, but also to cover up the bottom half of the holster so that you can wear a slightly shorter cover garment. Since a speed cut or dropped and offset holster design will not help with drawing from an IWB, we rely on the holster's rake to ease the contortion required to lift a gun straight out of a holster.

The huge variety of IWBs sold illustrate the tremendous variations in rake, high- mid- or low-ride, as well as quite an imaginative variety of belt loop innovations, including one or two simple loops attached to the holster, belt loops that snap on to the holster for easy on or easy off, hooks that catch on the bottom of the belt, a wide loop with a slot cut down the center through which you can thread the trouser belt loop so that the gun cannot move forward or aft and more.

One of the most ingenious of these many variations is the tuckable holster. This design was created by journalist and firearms instructor Dave Workman of North Bend, WA,[10] who created an IWB holster with a belt loop attached to a

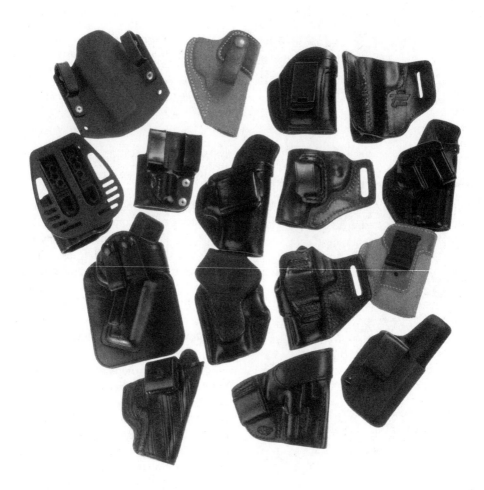

This collection of holsters demonstrates the variety of belt loops and attachments.

Dave Workman's original design, the first tuckable holster is still sold by D&D Gunleather. Photo courtesy of Dave Workman

stiff leather strip sewn to the base of the holster. Though he called his version the "Undershirt," Workman agreed to let Mitch Rosen's Extraordinary Gunleather reproduce the design, and market it as "The Workman," in honor of the inventor. Before long, other holster makers appropriated the tuckable holster concept and the design flowered. Today, nearly every holster maker has a tuckable design.

A tuckable holster is a radical and liberating concept for armed citizens who generally conceal a gun and holster beneath a shirt or vest that is loose and worn open at the bottom with the hem untucked. With a tuckable design, you can instead tuck your shirt tail between the body of the holster and its belt loops, all of which are concealed inside your waistband. This conceals extra well with a full-cut blouse of a patterned or textured fabric. My friend, Kathy Jackson, the former editor of *Concealed Carry Magazine*, swears by tuckable holsters. She conceals her Glock 26 beneath an ordinary blouse, and then adds a short, light or frilly vest or shirt as a top layer to enhance concealment. The combination allows enjoyment of many more feminine fashion options than dressing in loose untucked shirts and wearing vests. In addition, she enjoys the security of knowing that a gust of wind or inadvertent motion will not expose her concealed handgun, since it is buried beneath several covering layers.

An unsung yet very important characteristic of the tuckable holster is how low it sits inside the waistband. Only the grips of the gun are exposed, and then only as much as needed to accomplish a good drawing grip. For women in particular, the lower the holster can sit on the waistline, the more comfortable it is likely to be on the shorter female torso. Other IWB designs use belt loops that are attached to the holster only at the top so that they flop over the trouser waistband where you slip the belt through the loops.

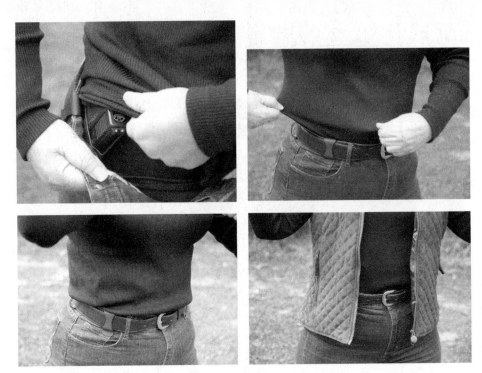

Kathy Jackson demonstrates a tuckable holster, worn over a thin chemise, but covered with a ribbed sweater that conceals better if fluffed out away from the gun a little. The entire ensemble is covered by a slim quilted vest.

CROSS DRAW HOLSTERS

Cross draw holsters comprise yet another type of holster to consider. Some of the IWB and OWB holsters you may find are designed to be carried forward of the weak-side hip. When drawing from a cross draw rig, the strong hand reaches across the stomach to grab the gun grips and pull the gun from the holster. The grips are easy to access because the holster holds the gun in roughly a 35-45-degree angle up and cross body. The downside of this carry position is the ease with which an assailant can jam your arm against your body and prevent access to your gun.

Because cross draw holsters are carried forward of the hip, this mode of concealed carry requires either a closed-fronted garment that is loose enough to pull up and entirely off the gun, much as is required by appendix carry. In fact, it simply is appendix carry moved to the opposite side of the abdomen.

Because the gun muzzle points outboard and does not point at any part of the body, cross draw carry may be a little safer than strong-side appendix carry; there simply is less anatomy that has to be considered when drawing and holstering the gun. At the same time, however, the negative feature of cross draw holsters is that, while the wearer is safer during drawing and reholstering, anyone else standing to

their weak side definitely is not! The angle at which the gun comes out of the holster bears most of the blame; most cross draw holsters position the gun at roughly a 45-degree orientation to the horizon. That's why many firearms schools disallow cross draw holsters. There is only one single location on the firing line where it is safe to draw and holster in a cross draw position: at the very end of the firing line in the direction in which the cross draw points the muzzle.

A neutral-rake cross draw holster is free of the drawing and holstering safety concerns, but these are rare and you will still need to convince your instructor or the range

The first step to drawing safely from a cross draw holster is clearing away a closed-front cover garment in what has been dubbed the Hackathorn Rip technique.

safety officer running the firing line that you can use it without pointing the muzzle anywhere but at the floor and downrange. Still, it can be done. Just as with complete focus on safety, you can draw and reholster in an appendix carry holster, but it does require a higher degree of attention to safety, as the potential for pointing the gun at your body is far greater than with a holster worn just behind the hip.

If there is one time in our gunhandling during which we are most at risk to violate the safety mandate against ever pointing a gun at yourself or others, holstering is that time. The gun muzzle needs to come to the holster pointing away from the body as the muzzle tip goes inside the holster mouth. When the muzzle enters the holster, tip the gun to match the line of the holster and slide it down to seat in the holster.

Your finger must come off the trigger as soon as you have decided not to shoot, and pause to be doubly certain you have moved your trigger finger far away from the gun before even approaching the holster. If your gun has an exposed hammer, your thumb can further block the hammer while you holster the gun, as Massad Ayoob teaches in his classes, although this safeguard is very gun-specific and will not prevent a striker-fired gun from discharging.

APPENDIX CARRY

Armed citizens aren't much different from other consumers. Trends come on strong, and then wane in popularity only to rise again. Appendix carry is once again on the rise among armed citizens of both genders. This horrifies many, because we read and hear armed citizens assert that because appendix carry is very fast from which to draw, is quite concealable and surprisingly comfortable, its practitioners are shockingly willing to accept the risk of pointing their handgun at their groin and genitalia in order to carry and conceal a handgun there.

While women have fewer anatomical features about which to worry, in appendix carry we still must exercise great care not to point the muzzle toward the lower abdomen or a leg below the holster while drawing and holstering. Of greater concern to women is the potential for an early gun discharge that may strike the femoral artery immediately after the trigger guard has cleared the holster but is not yet pointed at the target or assailant. This can be avoided during training and practice by never, ever drawing while seated or bending over. I'm less optimistic in real life, where armed defense may become necessary while seated in a car, leaning over to shield your head, running vigorously, knocked on your back with your legs bent as you try to avoid a blow or regain your feet. Though we train with great seriousness to never put the finger on the trigger until the gun is pointed into a target and we intend to shoot, much has been reported about the interruption of sequential actions and other confusion that occurs during and immediately after a life and death fight.

How likely is it that these dangers would converge on one emergency moment? Who can say? Certainly each element of our safe holstering procedure—indexing the trigger finger away from the trigger and trigger guard, controlling muzzle direction during holstering, blocking the hammer when your gun type accommodates this safeguard—protects against a fraction of a fraction of the dangers inherent in holstering guns.

Consider this: most armed citizens will go through their entire life without ever drawing a gun to thwart a violent criminal. Of the fraction who find the necessity of armed self defense thrust upon them, another fraction will not be standing upright. Dynamic shooting conditions comprise a larger piece of the "likelihood pie" than the fraction representing armed citizens who will use their guns in self defense. Setting up a situation that increases the risk instead of diminishes it is why so many worry about the safety of appendix carry. These serious compromises should only be considered when all other safer concealed carry options have been honestly tested and discarded for legitimate reasons.

From the positive viewpoint, strong side appendix carry is very concealable and it provides a reasonably quick draw stroke when the gun is carried at a completely neutral rake or angle just forward of the strong side hip. A fairly short-barreled handgun works best in appendix carry, since a four- or five-inch barrel is likely to poke into the upper thigh when you sit down, and the lower slung trouser waistband of modern fashions only exacerbates this because a gun and holster will sit as much as one to two inches lower than they do when carried on a belt at the true waistline.

Women with figures that have an extreme difference between the waist measurement and the measurement of the hips struggle to find a belt holster that can be comfortably fit atop that radical curve between waist and hip. On these figures, the relative flat of the abdomen gives a place that will accommodate a holstered gun, either carried in the appendix or cross draw position in either IWB or a holster attached outside the waistband. Ladies with very curvy or heavier figures sometimes declare that the appendix position is the only place they can carry an IWB holster.

Neutral holster rake is most useful for appendix carry because it positions the grips of the gun beneath the bust line where the natural fall of a blouse creates very good concealment. A muzzle-forward-raked holster will generally extend the grips of all but the smallest .380 beyond the natural line of the rib-cage, ruining concealment. A muzzle-back rake is all but impossible to grip and draw without considerable contortion of the forearm and wrist. Like Goldilocks' options, the neutral rake is "just right" for appendix carry.

SECURITY

Holster security can have two meanings. The first is the kind of high-level concealment we enjoy from a deeply concealed IWB holster like the tuckables we just discussed. The other type of security concerns how well the holster holds the gun until it is drawn. This is an issue requiring the holster designer to walk the tightrope of accessibility for quickly drawing the gun from a relatively concealed position, balanced against the absolute necessity that the gun must remain inside the holster, even if the holster is upside down. The holster may be upside

down if the armed citizen is knocked down in the course of an attack, rolls around on the floor while playing with pets or children, is involved in an accident or simply slips and falls on ice or down the stairwell.

A holster securely retains when the material the holster is made of is molded to closely match the contours

Rolling around on the floor with kids and dogs sometimes calls for extra-good retention. Here, Jennie wears a Bianchi CarryLok™ holster so her Springfield EMP is extra-well protected even if playtime with her Newfoundland, Cedar, gets too lively.

of the gun it will carry. That means the holster will have a slight indentation to grip the semi-auto pistol's ejection port or contour of the revolver's cylinder, and will be just slightly concave over the trigger guard, as well. Some manufacturers add a retention strap or a mechanical hook that locks onto the front of the trigger guard. Most mechanical retention devices release the gun with the press of a lever. A retention strap is a simpler security measure that the shooter disengages by either unsnapping or separating a Velcro® connection.

Take care that the retention device does not interfere with other aspects of safe gun operation. An OWB holster called the SERPA gained prominence in years past. It required the shooter to depress a button or lever right over the trigger guard. The trigger finger subsequently pushed toward the trigger as the gun came out of the

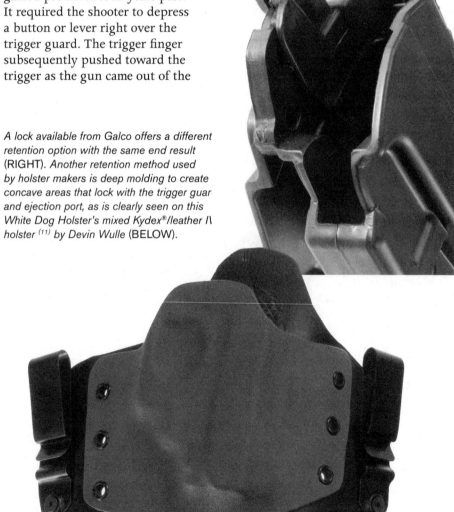

A lock available from Galco offers a different retention option with the same end result (RIGHT). Another retention method used by holster makers is deep molding to create concave areas that lock with the trigger guar and ejection port, as is clearly seen on this White Dog Holster's mixed Kydex®/leather I\ holster [11] by Devin Wulle (BELOW).

Another method of assuring that the gun stays in the holster is the thumb break strap, so called because the strap snaps to a back piece against which the shooter presses to open the snap prior to drawing from the holster.

holster unless the shooter was very nimble, indeed. Discharging the gun immediately after it was drawn but before it was yet pointed toward the target was a source of considerable concern about this design's safety. Investigations into and prohibitions on its use by the Federal Law Enforcement Training Center resulted. [12] At the time of this writing, SERPAs are still sold, but I am hard-pressed to recommend them.

A retention holster becomes especially critical if you carry your handgun openly, as is done by practitioners of open carry. When the gun is clearly visible to the public, a retention holster provides a margin of safety against a gun-grab attack by a criminal who intends to steal the gun or realizes that he must first disarm the armed citizen before committing another crime. The largest class of open carry practitioners, of course, is our nation's police forces. Police retention holsters have become very sophisticated, and drawing from a holster with level two or three retention entails two to three steps to disengage multiple retention devices, some of which can only be accomplished from the angle of the person wearing the belt from which the holster hangs, to foil grabs from the side or front. If open carrying, armed citizens need to practice the same degree of caution as does law enforcement.

Drawing a Ring's Blue Gun from an older Blackhawk SERPA holster demonstrates how close the finger used to release the SERPA lock comes to the trigger during the draw stroke.

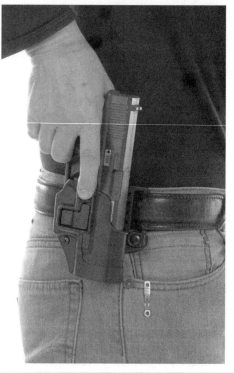

SAFETY COMES FIRST

While gun safety is paramount during any drawing and holstering steps, it is especially critical in appendix carry, in which it is all too easy to point the muzzle at the femoral artery when drawing or holstering. Never holster while seated, and if at all possible avoid drawing from that position if you carry in the appendix position. When drawing, take care to step back with the strong side leg to remove any body parts from the line of fire. The necessity of drawing or reholstering under stress and in body postures where the femoral artery is beneath the muzzle is a serious consideration that the armed citizen has to weigh against the concealability and comfort of their favorite concealed handgun carry spot.

The laser sights many attach to a defensive handgun are useful for a lot of things, including testing your safety during holstering. Activate the laser, and with a gun triple checked to assure it is unloaded, do a dozen draw and holster strokes in front of a mirror. If you see the dot of the aiming laser light up any part of your body while drawing or holstering, adjust the angle at which you return the gun to the holster, or make other changes, including where the holster sits on your belt. If you cannot draw and holster the gun without pointing the muzzle at part of your body, switch to a holster you can use more safely.

> *If you cannot draw and holster the gun without pointing the muzzle at part of your body, switch to a holster you can use more safely.*

Our biggest concern is the ability to be able to train and practice in 100 percent flawlessly-executed safety from the holster in which we will carry a loaded gun. That means starting out slowly drawing and reholstering an empty gun and only picking up speed when you have proven that you can draw and holster without pointing the muzzle at any part of your body. When you can do that, use dry fire to memorize and habituate that exact sequence and motions of drawing and returning the gun to the holster, increasing speed as the drill becomes smoother. Later, be sure you practice the same movements when you shoot at the range. Enroll in formal firearms training to put your gun, holster and skills to the test in a variety of situational drills, including moving, and drawing and firing from disadvantaged positions like being knocked down. Everything you do with your defense gun in practice, fun and training is the foundation for the very same motions you will execute when life is on the line. Do not form habits that will betray you and put you at risk for a self-inflicted gunshot wound.

NO FITTING ROOMS IN THE HOLSTER STORE

The toughest part of holster shopping is that it is virtually impossible in most retail gun stores to try out a variety of holsters. Sometimes you can remove the holster from its packaging and hold it against the location where you would carry it, but many store clerks will draw the line at letting you putting a holster on your belt, and there certainly isn't any safe way in a store to test holsters' wearability, let alone try a few draw and fire cycles from the holsters in stock with your own gun. After all, would you feel safe in a gun store in which several customers had guns out, drawing and holstering in the aisles? If you have a really warm relationship with a gun shop owner, you might be allowed to take a small selection of the holsters to a back room, unload your gun and try them out, but few are on such good terms with their local gun retailer.

This is another reason I strongly recommend saving up until you can budget for a holster set from a custom holster maker who expresses his or her willingness to work with your particular needs. Until you can, here is an effective alternative: Make friends among the people at your local gun club or shooting range, or join a shooting league, and ask if some of your fellow shooters would like to get together to try out each others' holsters. Most people who carry a concealed handgun own half a dozen holsters or more. Some of these were not returnable because, by the time their faults became apparent, scuffs or other wear made it unreasonable to ask a retailer to accept them as a return, so they went into a box or bag never again to see the light of day. In other instances, the owner no longer carries the gun for which a particular holster was purchased. There are lots of reasons that a holster ends up not being used.

In arranging a holster sharing session, you aren't necessarily looking for the exact holster you want to eventually buy. Use the opportunity, instead, to identify design elements about various holsters that work well for you, and if you could cobble them all together would comprise a perfect concealment rig for your particular needs. Once you know what you need, find that "cobbler," a holster maker who will make what you specify.

Some years ago, I led a women's study group in conjunction with one of my family's businesses, The Firearms Academy of Seattle, Inc. [13] Our first women's study group meeting was a holster fashion show. I was really pleased to notice on the Internet that a group of ladies in New York held just such an event in the summer of 2012, so the idea probably wasn't unique to us. It is heartening to know that ladies are getting together and sharing their experiences with guns, holsters and concealment clothing options. Your sharing session doesn't need to be that formal. People who practice concealed carry almost always have a little collection of cast-off holsters. Who knows? After the try-it-on session, you might turn the get-together into an informal swap meet!

WHAT WORKS?

What are some of the holster characteristics that work for most women? The first is a carry position that keeps the holster and any part of the gun from pressing into the iliac crest of the hipbone, and as much as possible, keeps the grips from jabbing into the ribcage. As we've discussed, this means the gun will be carried just forward of the hip or just behind the hip. Go too far behind the hip toward the small of the back, and the grips will catch your shirt or jacket when you sit or lean over and reveal your gun.

Depending on how high the holster sits and the dimensions of the handgun, a gun carried at a neutral rake is pretty much guaranteed to dig into the hip or the rib cage. A deep muzzle-back rake contributes a lot to comfort without sacrificing concealability. A muzzle-forward rake also works well in assuring comfortable carry for small handguns.

Holster height is also important because the fundamental reason we carry handguns for personal defense is the possibility that one day we may be compelled to draw the gun to stop a violent assailant. To do this most efficiently, we need to be able to lift the gun out of the holster with minimum upper body contortion, and for most women that adds the requirement that the mouth of the holster sit as low on the belt as possible, within the constraints of concealability.

I wish I could tell you to go out and find one perfect holster, but that is not how owning guns and holsters for concealed carry usually works out. I do believe that you can limit the number of unserviceable holsters you buy and discard by first defining the holster characteristics that you need, based on your individual figure, the handgun you wish to conceal, and the types of fashions under which you will be carrying your concealed handgun.

If you lead a life filled with different activities, you may find it necessary to expand your carry methods beyond one perfect belt holster, adding one alternative carry location like a shoulder, ankle or garter/thigh holster, and perhaps an additional option like a waist pack or holster handbag. In the following chapters, we'll evaluate these alternatives, studying their concealability, safety, security and functionality.

---

(1) Mitch Rosen Extraordinary Gun Leather, ibid, Nancy Special women's holster

(2) Galco International ibid., Stinger OWB holster

(3) International Defensive Pistol Association (IDPA), 2232 CR 719, Berryville, AR 72616, 870-545-3886, info@ idpa.com, http://www.idpa.com/

(4) International Practical Shooting Confederation (IPSC), P. O. Box 972, Oakville, Ontario, Canada L6K 0B1 http://www.ipsc.org/

(5) FIST, Inc., 20 Jay St., Ste 211, Brooklyn, NY 11201, 800-443-3478, fist98@aol.com http://www.fist-inc.com/hybrid.htm

(6) Comp-Tac Victory Gear, P.O. Box 1809, Spring, Texas 77383-1809, 281-209-3040

(7) Blade Tech Industries, 5530 184th St E, Suite A, Puyallup, WA 98375, 877-331-5793, http://www.blade-tech.com/Black-Ice-DOH-pr-1211.html

(8) Kramer Handgun Leather, ibid.

(9) Ted Blocker Holsters, ibid.

(10) Dave Workman's D & D Gunleather, P.O. Box 1638, North Bend, WA 98045, www.danddgunleather.com/

(11) White Dog Holsters, http://www.whitedogholsters.com/ or via email devin@whitedogholsters.com

(12) FLETC study on SERPA holster dangers: www.fletc.gov/reference/public-information/freedom-of-information-act-foia/reading-room/training-information/holisterStudy.pdf/download

(13) The Firearms Academy of Seattle, Inc., P. O. Box 400, Onalaska, WA 98570 360-978-6100, www.firearmsacademy.com

CLASSIC NON-BELT HOLSTERS

There was a time when the word "holster" meant a simple, belt-mounted leather scabbard like those discussed in the last chapter. Nowadays "holster" could also mean a shoulder holster or an ankle holster. It could be a loose pouch in a shape that only approximates the lines of the gun it holds. It might have a retention strap, a catch that holds the gun by the trigger guard until released, or tight molding that holds the gun inside the holster. It could be made of leather, fabric or Kydex®, a thermoplastic material. Our options are only limited by our imagination and by what is safe.

Envision a female human body. What areas do clothing that is loose enough to hide a handgun beneath conventionally cover? What areas are easily reached with the hands? Hmmm, that disqualifies the head, neck, arms, shoulders and much of the back. That still leaves a lot of real estate on which to conceal a gun! Not surprisingly, holster manufacturers make concealed carry products exploiting nearly all of the likely—and many of the unlikely—concealment positions.

Like much else that we've discussed, each of the various handgun concealment positions has strong points and weak points. Some accommodate safe practice and training in situations where other shooters are nearby, while some do not. Some position the gun much more accessibly than others and some are subject to the danger that an assailant can too easily block you from drawing the gun. Often these pros and cons seem to have nearly equal weight. Some are designed for maximum concealment while others make it less likely that someone will bump into your handgun. Some are more comfortable for long hours of wear than others. Some expose the gun to the danger of being grabbed and taken away while others have the risk that it is easier for an assailant to prevent you from reaching it and drawing your gun. Finally—and this is important—some are safer and some more dangerous because drawing and holstering a gun from some

Author assumes a pose from Leonardo DaVinci's Vitruvian Man drawing, with holsters and guns in all the possible carry places. Included are the Flashbang bra holster (concealed for obvious reasons), shoulder holster, belly band (also hidden) holster on strong side appendix carry, and holster right behind the strong side hip, cross draw on weak side, thigh/garter holster, ankle holster, holster purse on strong side, plus a waistpack and a holster purse. Were the shooter left handed, all these positions would simply be reversed, as if viewed in a mirror.

locations results in pointing the gun at part of your anatomy, while many others do not. Read that last sentence again, please.

The necessity of assuring that the gun can be safely drawn and safely returned to the holster is a strong rationale for using belt holsters. The muzzle of a gun carried in a belt holster generally points down, and since humans are bipedal, when standing there is just less of us to be harmed should the gun discharge when pointing in that direction. Even so, when using a belt holster, opportunities to unsafely point the gun at yourself or another will arise, so you must adhere to impeccable safety procedures.

We covered belt holsters in the previous chapter, and, though it saddens me, I acknowledge that some readers have already written off carrying in a belt holster for a variety of personal reasons. Still, these ladies need safe ways to carry a concealed handgun for self defense. Let us, then, search until we identify the safest alternative methods to carry a personal protection handgun.

As we study non-traditional holsters, our first priority has to be identifying ways to safely use holsters in these alternative locations. Some of the solution lies in strict user-enforced protocols with unrelenting caution to insert the loaded gun into the holster without ever pointing at yourself or another human being. Test any new holster with extensive dryfire practice, using a mirror, and when possible a laser sight, to reveal exactly where the muzzle points when drawing the gun and returning it to the holster.

Using a nonconventional concealment rig may require setting up safety zones so you can get the gun safely into the carry rig, and then put the rig on your body. Ask yourself, though, how you are going to use this holster if you must bring the gun out in public. At some point, the gun will need to go back into the holster, and if you have just averted a life-threatening danger, you will be under the effect of adrenaline and must expect a considerable loss of manual dexterity, tremors and reduced sensation in extremities. This is no condition to try inserting a loaded gun back into a holster or carry device that is only marginally safe under the best of circumstances.

You may find safe ways that, though cumbersome and time-consuming, let you use the holster safely. With creativity and integrity (safety is not a practice upon which self-delusion is acceptable) the determined armed citizen can often work out safety protocols to allow use of non-belt holsters. In the pages to follow, we'll review some of the more common types.

SHOULDER HOLSTERS

The entertainment industry seems to love the shoulder holster, probably because it keeps the gun in the picture frame. Of course, actual concealment isn't required on the silver screen; the challenge of genuinely concealing a gun in a shoulder holster is a little more demanding than the entertainment industry portrays.

First, if considering a shoulder holster, make sure that the gun and holster blend with the lines of the torso. Most shoulder holsters carry the gun with the grips down and the barrel horizontal, muzzle pointing to the rear. This design, typified by the Miami Classic rig of 1980s TV fame, is relatively easy from which to draw, unless an assailant gets close

Be aware that clothing must sit high enough on the neck and shoulders to conceal the shoulder holster's harness.

enough to block your drawing arm against your body before you can get the gun oriented toward the aggressor.

Many women's bodies aren't thick enough from front to back that the muzzle end of the holster does not poke into the back of their shirt or jacket, and nothing short of a heavy, down-filled coat will disguise it. A few manufacturers sell shoulder holsters that suspend the gun beneath your arm with the muzzle down and the grips forward where they are easy to grasp. With a full-cut

When drawing, take care to lift the non-dominant hand and arm high above the path the gun travels during the draw stroke to avoid pointing a gun at your own arm, as demonstrated with Ring's Blue Gun (LEFT)! You might accomplish that by lifting your non-dominant arm above the gun.

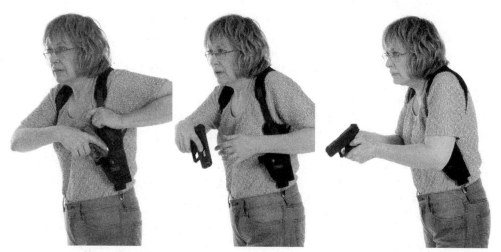

If it is helpful, grasp the shoulder holster harness above the holster (gripped through your jacket during concealment) to assure your hand remains above the gun and does not come down to the body's midline until the gun is extended beyond.

bloused jacket, like a leather bomber jacket, these conceal fairly well, even on thinner women. Take care with the concealment jacket, however, because if the fit is too tailored, you will definitely look chunkier on the gun side. Finally, premier holster craftsman Rusty Sherrick [1] has reintroduced the muzzle-up shoulder holster design for the snub-nosed revolver. He alleviates safety concerns by positioning the holster so the muzzle points in front of the armpit.

Shoulder holsters are suspended on several varieties of harnesses. Most shoulder rigs are donned like a vest, since the harness is worn across both shoulders. The gun hangs below the weak side armpit, and usually a balancing pouch for ammunition hangs under the opposite armpit. For smaller, lighter guns, Galco makes the elegantly minimal Executive Shoulder Holster, [2] which only suspends a holstered gun from straps across one shoulder without the balancing weight of ammunition on the other side.

Because the shoulder holster does not have the solid support of the waistband and a belt, often an elasticized strap that is much like men's suspenders or braces with a clip at the end secures the rig to your belt or waistband. This helps to limit any flopping around the rig may do when you walk or run. Other designs incorporate an elasticized strap around the torso to stabilize the holster. In addition, shoulder holsters usually include a security strap or several snaps that make sure that the gun remains inside the holster.

If considering a shoulder holster, it would be wise to borrow one from a friend or shooting companion and try wearing it for one or two days. You may find that the weight on the trapezius muscles atop your shoulders becomes unbearable, so giving this system a test run before spending hundreds of dollars to buy your own makes sense, whether that means borrowing or buying a very low end rig primarily for test purposes. Shoulder holsters may or may not be your best option.

WAY DOWN ON THE ANKLE

The other predominant non-belt style holster is the ankle holster. Carrying a defense handgun on an ankle is dependent on trouser fashions, the legs of which are sometimes straight or full or flaired. Trouser length is also critical, as is the way that you sit so that the inside of your non-dominant side ankle remains covered by the fabric of the pants leg. Sitting with crossed legs, for example, causes the trouser leg to ride up more than sitting with both feet on the floor, plus crossing your legs eliminates the possibility of camouflaging the gun and holster bulk by keeping both ankles close together.

When wearing casual shoes, one of the best camouflage techniques for an ankle holster is wearing two stockings. The inner stocking protects your skin from abrasion by the holster or the grips of the gun. A lot of ankle holsters are backed by soft neoprene, wool felt or sheepskin, but the pistol grips usually protrude above those cushioning materials. Besides, nothing is quite as comfortable as a soft stocking next to the skin. After you put on the ankle holster and cinch its band nice and tight, and then pull a larger, somewhat bulky stocking over the very top. Because there is so much movement from walking, being able to tighten the band of the ankle holster is essential. Otherwise, the movement will rub open sores after just one day of wear.

Another impediment to ankle holsters for women is the thinner joints of the female body relative to the male body. A gun and ankle holster that would conceal beneath a fellow's Levi®s may create a noticeable bulge on a lady's leg. Trousers of a fairly stiff fabric will help, as will a straight or wide-legged trouser design.

Most carry an ankle holster on the inside of the non-dominant side leg. I have known people who purported to carry on the outside of the ankle, but they must be possessed of considerably greater grace than I can muster, because that position is continually banging into door frames, chair, table and desk legs, and seems more difficult to conceal, as well. My advice is to follow the larger numbers who put the ankle holster on the inside of the non-dominant side ankle.

From this carry location, drawing from a standing position can be accomplished by dropping into a deep crouch, pulling up on the trouser fabric at the knee and drawing the gun with the dominant hand. In fast-breaking circumstances, it is entirely possible to simply take the shot from the crouch while rising in preparation to stand up, back up, run away or whatever other movement the situation demands. Indeed, it is the necessity of movement during a self-defense emergency that costs the ankle holster the most points when it's suitability for self defense is being evaluated. It is a simple thing to draw from a belt holster while at a full-speed run–ask any competitive shooter–but the same is not true for ankle holsters. Drawing from an ankle holster at even a slow and deliberate walk is simply not possible.

People in certain jobs or circumstances are more likely to need a gun while seated, and this may include drivers and folks who work seated in very confined

The two-stocking ankle rig camouflage and comfort carry method.

spaces, to identify only two possible scenarios. A comfortable ankle holster worn beneath straight-legged trousers is sometimes more accessible than a belt holster that can become entangled beneath a seat belt or from which drawing may be impeded by the arm of an office chair. In these situations, the ankle holster really comes into its own.

In addition, some armed citizens use an ankle holster to carry a second, last-ditch gun. If their primary gun fails or they are blocked, knocked to the ground or unable to get a hand on their primary gun, it may be possible to lift the ankle until it is close enough to the hand to draw the gun and fight back.

Like all skills, practice is required to bring draw and fire speeds up to par, remembering that the assailant usually has initiated the fight and, if drawing a gun in real life, you are in all likelihood putting everything you've got into regaining control of the situation. You can get in a lot of meaningful drawing practice in dry-fire with an unloaded gun. This self-training is particularly enhanced by laser sights which help confirm that the draw stroke you are habituating is indeed safe, efficient and accurate.

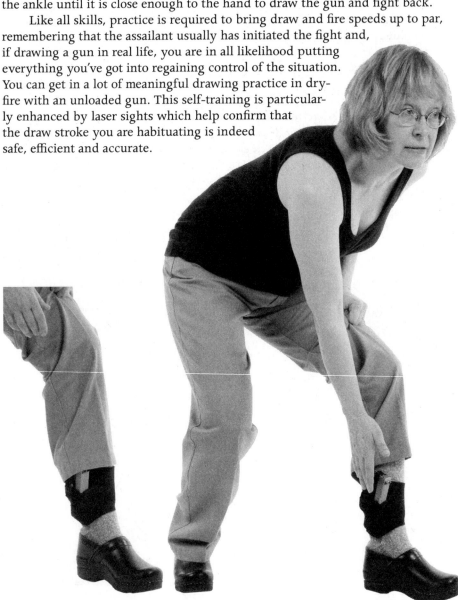

Drawing from an ankle holster.

DRYFIRE

Dryfire is the practice of going through all the steps of firing without any ammunition in the gun. The purpose of dryfire is to smooth out hesitation and program in smoothness and sure-handedness in the steps that precede firing, as Dave Spaulding so clearly explains in his book *Handgun Combatives*, as well as on his website of the same name[1].

Shooters also use dryfire to hone trigger control skills, and even use dummy rounds (inert ammunition cartridges) to perfect their reloading skills. For our purposes—to enhance concealed carry skills—let's concentrate on using dryfire to refine the steps of moving clothing out of the way, establishing a good, firing grip on the handgun, drawing it from the holster without snagging or tangling in clothing, and presenting it on target so that the sights are lined up and you are ready to take an accurate shot.

Dryfire is recommended because it is the only way many self-defense gun owners can enjoy regular handgun practice on a daily basis. Dryfire is the bridge that lets many skilled self-defense practitioners maintain and perfect skills like drawing from a holster so that the time spent at the firing range and using expensive ammunition is more productive.

Dryfire is strongly recommended, but only for those who will approach it with complete seriousness and focus on doing it safely. This practice has many benefits and one risk of considerable gravity. Unsafe procedures may unintentionally mix live ammunition into the dry fire with catastrophic results. To overcome this hazard when we practice dryfire, we implement stringent safety rules from which we never deviate.

To safely practice dryfire, you must set up a secure practice area that is entirely free of any ammunition, and one that has a safe bullet-proof backstop toward which you can point the gun during the practice. In recognition of the potential for terrible mistakes, we rely on double and triple layers of precaution to assure safety. Only when safety is assured can we reap the benefits of dryfire practice. Bullet stopping backstops include Ravelin Group's (formerly known as Safe Direction)[2] ballistic containment panel, a three-foot tightly packed bookshelf filled with large volumes like the Encyclopedia Britannica or a shelf full of large phone books. Put up a target you can focus on that directs the muzzle into the area that is protected by the safe backstop material.

When starting a dryfire practice session, unload your handgun and put all ammunition and any other guns in a different room. Triple check the chamber(s) and on a semi-automatic, the magazine and magazine well to guarantee that the gun is entirely unloaded. Because dryfire is generally conducted at home where this kind of gunhandling would be incredibly unsafe, say out loud so you can hear your words, "This is dryfire. The gun is unloaded." Verify one last time that this is true and the gun is indeed unloaded.

Blade Tech Industries' Training Barrel[3] is an excellent accessory for use during dryfire, since you replace your semi-automatic's actual barrel with a plastic replica into which no ammunition can be loaded, because a solid block of plastic sits where the barrel's chamber would usually be. If available for your model of semi-automatic handgun, the Training Barrel adds a valuable layer of safety to dryfire practice.

Use the handy Safe Direction Academy dryfire pad, or if you can, a Kevlar® panel from a bullet-resistant vest that has been surplussed.

Dryfire is only as effective as your level of concentration on the skills being practiced, so it should only be conducted when no one else is around to distract you. The only exception is including an associate who is serving as a coach. They must also participate in the dryfire ritual.

During dryfire, keep your mind on what you are doing! Limit practice sessions to five or ten minutes so that you can maintain a total focus on the skills being practiced. If your attention wanders or you are called away from the practice, you must reinitiate the practice session by checking to be sure there is no ammunition in the room and triple-checking to be sure the gun is unloaded. If interrupted, it might be best to simply postpone dryfire practice until later when you can perform both the dryfire safety ritual and the practice routines with complete attention to the practice.

Most dryfire-related gun accidents occur because the armed citizen loses his or her focus on safe practice and brings a loaded magazine or ammunition into the practice area, or loads the gun for personal protection when interrupted, then fails to go through the safety routine

Women at the Firearms Academy of Seattle range study gun safety with demonstrations using their own carry ammo, testing home-made safety areas like a fully packed bookshelf.

Dryfire preparation requires triple checking the gun's condition, verifying that it is unloaded by both a visual check and a tactile check.

before returning to the dryfire practice. Do not fall prey to inattention! If you cannot keep your mind on dryfire practice, postpone the practice until you can.

When you quit dryfire, whether that is because you are done practicing or you have been interrupted, you must put in place safeguards to prevent picking up the gun for additional dryfire practice without verifying that it is unloaded. If, after dryfire, you need to holster and carry the gun for personal protection, load it and immediately holster it, while saying out loud, "Practice is over. This gun is loaded," and repeat the message several times emphatically. After holstering the gun, do not handle it again unless it is required for immediate self defense. If your circumstances don't require a loaded defense gun, it will be safer if you

Replacing the gun's barrel with a device like Blade Tech's dryfire replacement barrel increases safety tremendously.[3]

can put the gun in the gun safe and lock it away for an hour or two after dryfire practice so you don't pick it up for just a little more practice outside of the safety of the dry fire practice in an ammunition-free area.

Dryfire practice is an important skill building and skill maintenance tool. It is especially important to those who carry in unconventional holsters because of the difficulty obtaining safe training and practice in drawing from anything but a belt holster in training classes. Even for armed citizens who carry a gun in a belt holster, practicing is difficult because of the stringent prohibitions against drawing from holsters that are enforced at most public shooting ranges. For those who live in heavily urban areas where your only options for shooting practice are indoor ranges where drawing from a holster is often prohibited, dryfire practice is also a useful way to keep up skills between formal classes.

(1) Handgun Combatives, Dave Spaulding, http://www.handguncombatives.com

(2) Steve and Kate Camp, Ravelin Group, LLC, 426 S. Westgate, Suite S-1, Addison, IL 60101, 630-834-4423, www.ravelingroup.com

(3) Blade Tech Industries, 5530 184th St E Suite A Puyallup, WA 98375, 877-331-5793, http://www.blade-tech.com/Training-Barrel-pr-1018.html

NON-TRADITIONAL HOLSTERS

Pocket holsters, bra holsters, garter holsters and belly-band holsters—oh, my! These aren't holsters in the conventional sense of leather molded to match the shape of a gun, mounted to a belt, shoulder harness or ankle strap, but some are practical methods for carrying a concealed handgun. Let's discuss how to conceal a gun in non-traditional but on-body carry innovations and study how to draw safely from them.

With a growing concealed carry market, holster makers and entrepreneurs have introduced tremendous numbers of concealment products. As a result, concealed carry practitioners have so many options that it is sometimes hard to separate the concealment devices based on wishful thinking from practical, safe and user-friendly options. The law enforcement practice of discretely concealing a tiny back-up or hideout gun was the predecessor to many of the deep concealment methods currently in use. Today, I see an awful lot of private citizens carrying very small guns in nearly inaccessible locations that were originally conceived as ways to carry a gun for last-ditch defense if one's uniformed cohorts couldn't get there in time.

Have we forgotten why we carry self-defense guns? We carry guns because we may need to defend self or family from attack. If the necessity arises, it is very likely that things will happen extremely quickly, our hands may be full of shopping bags, or we may be concurrently protecting children or carrying an armload of books or other cargo. Let's keep accessibility in mind as we consider non-traditional holsters for concealed carry. Let's not add any unnecessary impediments to drawing the self-defense gun.

POCKET CARRY

Probably the most common nontraditional holster is the pocket holster. Made of leather, fabric, neoprene or other synthetic material, it is very much like a conventional belt holster, except that it has no belt loops and its outline when seen through the pocket is disguised to look like a smooth wallet or small notebook. The best pocket holsters have a somewhat sticky surface, like rough-side-out leather or a tacky rubber like finish, that makes the holster cling to the fabric inside the pocket so that when you draw the gun the holster remains behind and the gun comes out cleanly. Alternatively, a protruding corner on the pocket holster may hook inside the pocket so the gun comes out unimpeded, while other pocket holster designs let you push the holster off with your thumb when drawing.

Using a pocket holster requires somewhat larger pockets than are common on most women's jeans, but cargo

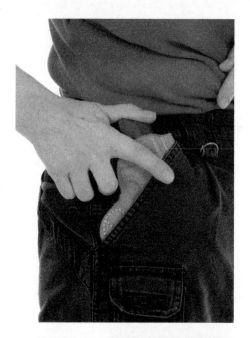

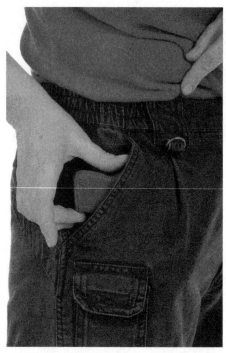

Using a pocket holster: first put the gun in the holster, then insert it into the pocket. If the fit is tight, that's a good thing, as it augurs well for the rig remaining in the pocket when you sit down and move around. (TOP) The pleats on these Royal Robbins hiking pants entirely hide the holstered gun from the front, and the depth of the pocket keeps it out of view from behind.

Various designs help keep the pocket holster and gun inside the pocket, including this older Ahern model on which the rough side of the leather holds the holster inside the pocket.

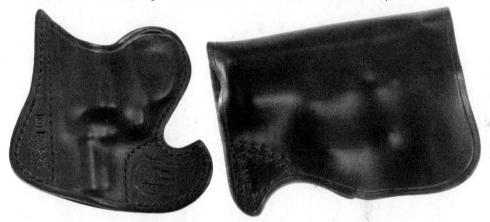

Don Hume and Kramer Handgun Leather models with a large hook below the trigger guard are designed to catch on the edge of the pocket as the gun is drawn.

DeSantis' pocket holster has sticky little silicone nubs that hold it in the pocket.

pants and some cotton twill slacks with pleated fronts and slash pockets will conceal a pocket-holstered gun. They work best with quite small and very light guns hidden in heavy clothing with large pockets. If the gun is too heavy, the weight of the holster and the gun can cause one side of the jacket or trousers to sag noticeably.

Make sure the holster holds the gun securely enough that when you are not standing upright, the gun cannot work its way out of the holster, and that the holster itself will stay inside the pocket. If carrying in a pocket frequently, sew a small tab of Velcro or a little snap along the top of trouser pockets to keep them discreetly closed while remaining easy to push open when your hand goes in your pocket to draw.

When needing to return the gun to a pocket holster, you must be able to

In a ground fight, the last thing you need is your gun coming out of your pocket, where the assailant who has already knocked you to the ground can grab for it.

holster it without pointing the muzzle at your support hand or the leg and foot below the pocket holster. The femoral artery's location makes this a particular concern, and pointing the muzzle at any part of your body during holstering is not acceptable. If you cannot holster the gun without pointing it at any part of yourself, you will need to use your non-gun hand to pull the pocket holster out, carefully slip it over the muzzle of the gun, then push the gun and holster back into the pocket together. Can you imagine executing that sequence of motions with your attention split between an assailant, onlookers, the assailant's compatriots and responding law enforcement? If not, you will understand why we keep carry methods like the pocket carry in reserve as secondary choices employed in tandem with a primary gun in a belt holster, or as a last ditch way to carry a defensive handgun.

Pocket holster advertising promotes the ability to have your hand on the grips of the gun in an unsure situation where the need for deadly force is possible but not immediately necessary, as would occur in a situation of escalating danger. When it is time to draw, the gun is drawn from its pocket holster much like a conventional belt holster. You will find certain pocket holster products that include a hole over the trigger so the gun can be fired without removing it from the holster. Since the pocket holster's main raison d'etre is to protect the trigger from inadvertent contact, you must carefully weigh the perceived advantage of being able to fire from a jacket pocket against the danger of a negligent discharge.

BELLY BANDS

Another old but proven deep concealment method is the belly band, usually a three- or four-inch wide band of elastic into which has been sewn "holster" pockets with a retention strap to secure a handgun. Usually, additional pockets are sewn for spare magazines, ID and other necessary items. These deep concealment rigs are very similar to the money belts tourists strap beneath clothing to avoid losing money and passports to pickpockets. Galco's Underwraps Belly Band [1] is constructed of two layers of elastic band stitched together, and has proven very durable and free of the tendency of a single layer of elastic to roll up at the edges.

Because they do not require a belt and work well beneath skirted suits, belly bands are popular with women and can work nicely concealed beneath even light, airy fabrics, or with sweat pants or pull-on workout shorts and other clothing that does not include a waistband to support a gun, holster and belt.

Because you can cinch up the elasticized belly band at pretty much any location on the torso, it can be used to carry a small handgun right beneath the bust-line, below the armpit, along the ribcage, just beneath the waistband of a skirt or pair of trousers, and most anywhere else up or down the torso as dictated by body shape or concealment clothing. This makes it easy to put the concealment gun close to the same position as your range practice holster even when you are not wearing belted trousers. The same steps for clearing away clothing and moving your hand to the grips of the gun can then apply to the pistol carried in the belly band. This isn't true for many other deep concealment methods.

As illustrated in the images, the worst downside for belly bands is that it is impossible to safely holster the gun once it is drawn. When putting on the rig, it is safest to put the gun in the belly band's sewn holster pocket, and then wrap the band containing the gun around the torso. The pocket closes up without a gun inside once the elastic is cinched around the torso, and it is not safe to pry the pocket open with the non-dominant hand's fingers preparatory to sticking the gun inside, since that puts the fingers in front of the muzzle.

If you need to safely get a gun drawn from a belly band out of your hands during a real-life emergency, you had better have another safe location available into which you can stow it, because with the loss of manual dexterity that is the natural result of adrenaline's fight-or-flight preparations, the dangers are very real that you will point a loaded

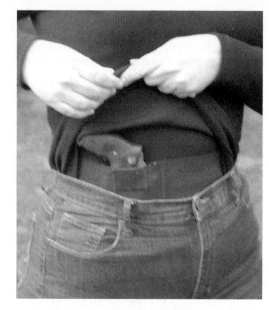

Kathy reveals a Gould & Goodrich belly band.

Don't do this! Take care, when putting a gun in a belly band, not to make this mistake, demonstrated here with a Ring's dummy gun. It is all too easy to pry the elastic layers apart before putting the gun in, and point the muzzle right at your own fingers as you try to get the gun into its elasticized pouch. Instead, either put the gun in the elastic holster before it is tightly cinched around your body, or find a way to pry open the elastic that keeps your fingers well away from the gun's muzzle.

pistol toward your body, at your lower extremities or at your non-gun hand's fingers while struggling to return it to the tight elasticized holster in the belly band.

Do not misunderstand—I am not arguing against carrying in a belly band. I am stressing the importance of working out in advance how you will get the gun out of your hands if you need to during conditions of extreme stress.

The belly band is often advertised as the perfect solution for concealed

carry when weather is too hot to wear a concealment shirt or vest. That tight elastic band can get pretty sweaty and uncomfortable against skin when worn all day in hot weather. My friend Kathy Jackson of Cornered Cat Training Company [2] recommends wearing a thin, soft cotton tube top beneath the belly band, where it does the same job as the base layer of a thin, soft stocking worn underneath an ankle holster discussed in the previous chapter.

Another belt-free carry option is the kangaroo pouch typified by the

Melissa starts this demo by showing how well the belly band concealed Glock 26 beneath a slim chemise covered by a pretty patterned chiffon blouse. To draw, she grabs the hem of both her blouse and chemise and gets a full grip on the gun, then lifts it straight up out of the sewn-in elastic holster.

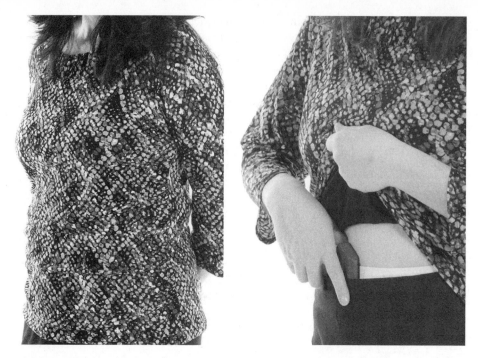

A KelTek P3AT in a SmartCarry™ pouch under the waistband of her skirt disappears beneath Melissa's vertically ruched blouse. To draw, she lifts the hem of her blouse, accessing the pistol in the SmartCarry™ pouch on a strap around her hips.

Smart Carry or Thunderwear brand of pouch holster.[3] A fabric pouch, covering the lower abdomen, is suspended from a strap slung low on the hips to carry a small handgun and a spare magazine. Some women have commented that the last thing they want is bulk that makes them look thicker through the lower body, but for others, this is a viable carry method that works beneath sweat pants and gathered skirts.

When putting on the kangaroo pouch holster, have the gun and spare magazine already in the pouch, then while standing up and being careful to keep the muzzle pointed away and in a safe direction, hang the pouch low on your hips and secure the hip strap, usually by connecting Velcro® that lets you attain a perfect fit. Put on your outer garment, be that trousers or a full skirt. So far, so good! Although the pouch is not elasticized, it is difficult to safely return the gun to the pouch's holster beneath clothing without prying the pockets open with your fingers, which puts them in front of the gun's muzzle. As with the belly band, if carrying in a kangaroo pouch holster, work out a safe alternative in which you can secure the gun if you have drawn it in self defense.

UNDERGARMENTS

Over the years, a great variety of holsters that attach to the wearer's brassiere have come and gone. Some were mere fabric pockets designed to attach to the side of the bra, others used the band beneath the bra cups as the supporting structure, and a few short-lived inventions purported to conceal a gun in bosom cleavage. Most of these must surely have been male fantasies, at least that is what I thought until Lisa Looper of Looper Law Enforcement LLC introduced the Flashbang holster.[4]

The Flashbang is a Kydex® clamshell holster suspended from the bra band, attached by a small strap going around the fabric between the bra cups. The muzzle of the gun is held tight against the body beneath the bra band or the un-derwire of the muzzle-side bra cup, and this keeps a small gun like a J-frame re-volver or one of the ultra-tiny .380s or 9mm semi-autos from flopping out during regular activity. Ladies report that it takes a little while to become accustomed to the muzzle end of the holster beneath the bra band or underwire, but they also say that they're surprised at how quickly they adjust and become comfortable with the carry method.

With a Flashbang holster the shirt is worn untucked. To draw, the hand slips under the shirt, up to the grips of the gun and pulls down sharply to click the gun out of the clamshell holster. The only safety concern I've seen is sweep-ing the non-dominant arm with the muzzle as the gun comes out of the clam-shell and before it can be oriented forward. This can be prevented by using the non-dominant hand to lift the clothing up and out of the way, holding the elbow high to be sure you don't inadvertently "muzzle" your arm, wrist or hand before the gun is pointed into the target. Alternatively, the arm could be thrust forward in a strike to back off an assailant, or moved to the side and back where it cannot be in the path of the muzzle. By incorporating that safety procedure, the Flash-bang holster provides a safe and very concealable gun carry method that lets women wear many of today's fashions and still carry a small gun.

Returning the gun to the Flashbang while it is on body requires the use of the non-dominant hand. It can be done, but great care is required so the muzzle doesn't point at the fingers or the rest of the arm. Lift the elbow high, make a wide, rounded "C" with

Lisa Looper displays the Flashbang holster at a firearms convention, where her invention earned a lot of attention.

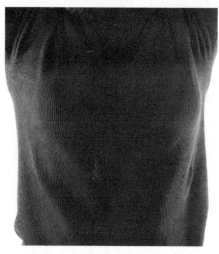

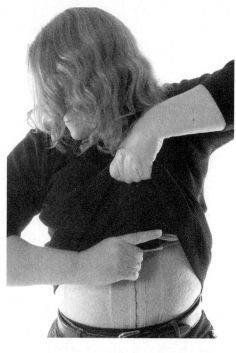

Kathy graciously provides a demonstration of safely drawing from a Flashbang holster. First, she demonstrates how even the stretch of upraised arms does not reveal the Glock 26 secured in the Flashbang holster, because of the drape of the sweater over the bust line. (TOP LEFT) As she starts the draw stroke, Kathy emphasized how important it is to lift the non-dominant arm out of harm's way (ABOVE RIGHT) before the gun comes out of the Flashbang's Kydex® clamshell holster. To draw, she lifts the sweater to clear access to the grips of the gun, gets a full shooting grip, and gives a sharp tug to free the pistol from the clamshell holster. (BELOW)

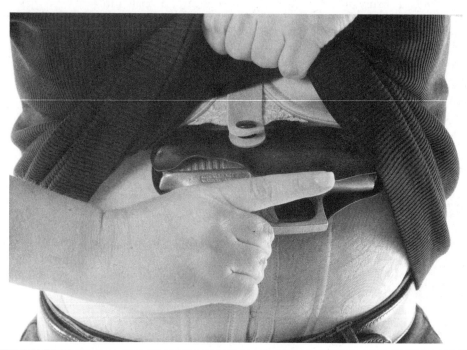

index finger and thumb to support the clamshell, and very slowly and carefully insert the muzzle of the gun, making sure your finger is far away from the trigger guard and that no clothing slips into the clamshell holster with the gun.

Learn how to safely get your gun into the Flashbang with either a Ring's Blue Gun casting or your own gun unloaded as if for the dryfire ritual we discussed earlier. After several hundred practice runs in which you have put the gun into the Flashbang without pointing the muzzle at your body, arm or fingers, find a day when no one else is at your gun club, and go through the holstering, drawing and firing steps at $\frac{1}{4}$ speed, $\frac{1}{2}$ speed and increasing speed only as you are able to do so safely. Having a friend along as safety observer is recommended.

Looper also invented a holster that attaches inside the side band of the brassiere and bra cup, which she dubbed the "Marilyn." She reports that in a sports bra, this is a very practical method for carrying a small gun during exercise like jogging, and her demonstrations of drawing from the Marilyn holster are smooth and fast.

The Flashbang and Marilyn holsters accommodate carrying a small gun beneath very feminine clothing that you probably previously thought entirely incompatible with concealed carry. That is wonderful and I'm greatly in favor of it. Still, I have to urge that you use this method only if you can draw and holster the gun without pointing the muzzle at your arm or hand. How tragic it would be if in defending yourself you maimed or injured yourself or a companion by inadvertently discharging the gun while drawing or putting it back in the holster.

Lisa Looper demonstrates drawing from the Marilyn holster. The wide neckline of Lisa's pullover gives great access to the small, flat semi-automatic in the holster attached beneath the side band of her brassiere.

UNDER A SKIRT

If you attached an ankle holster to a bigger band and moved it all above the knee, you'd essentially have a thigh holster. The term thigh holster actually describes two holster products: one, the tactical thigh rig worn on the outside of the thigh and created for use in full SWAT or tactical gear; the other, a deep concealment option, perhaps more accurately called a thigh band holster or sometimes called a garter holster. Some are made of the same wide heavy elastic as a belly band and others of soft, comfy neoprene, but sized to fit around the thigh and secured with large patches of Velcro®. Most come with the addition of a nylon waist strap and at least one garter, and often two, attached to the thigh band as insurance to keep it from slipping down. Unlike the belly band, which stops at the hips if it slips down, there is nothing but the tight elastic to keep the thigh band up without the garters.

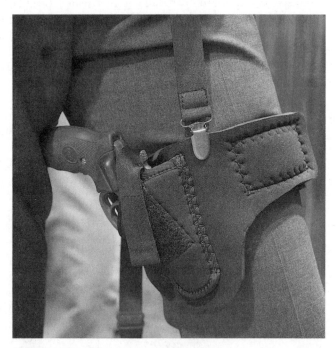

Thigh band holsters conceal nicely beneath dresses and skirts. I can't help but raise a skeptical eyebrow when I see demonstrations of thigh

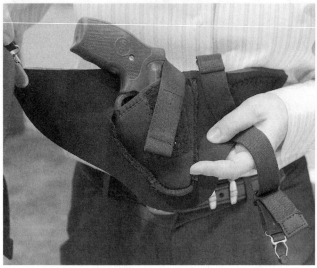

At a gun industry convention, the author tried out DeSantis Gunhide's newly introduced neoprene thigh holster. It has garters that attach to a waistband to support the gear. You'll need to let your imagination fill in how it would work over hosiery under a skirt!

band holsters positioned to the outside of the leg, and suspect this is done for comfort and not for concealment. A thigh band holster will conceal better on the inside of the thigh, where a skirt will hide the gun and holster quite nicely, and drawing is much more accessible from this position. Like so many holster options, comfort in a thigh band holster increases with wear and experience since adding the bulk and weight of even a small .380 seems hard to ignore at first. With practice you may become comfortable carrying a gun in this location and it can provide a very concealable option that will work well when you wear a dress.

When learning to draw from a thigh band holster, make careful observations of where the muzzle points when the gun comes out of the holster. If the muzzle points right at your knee or at your foot, alter the angle at which you draw so that the muzzle is oriented forward. Like other alternative carry methods, you will probably find that the only safe way to get your handgun into the thigh band holster is when the entire rig is off-body. Don't cheat and say, "Well, I'll just be extra careful as I pry the elastic open and slip my gun past my fingers." You may be able to do that under calm conditions, but find it disastrous when great danger has only recently passed and, full of adrenaline, your hands shake uncontrollably.

Melissa demonstrates drawing from Galco's thigh holster concealed beneath a skirt.

HOLSTER CLOTHING

In addition to the many concealment holsters, a considerable array of clothing to which holsters have been added is sold. Among the first of this concept to see widespread distribution was Greg Kramer's Undershirt holster [6]. It is a sleeveless undershirt made of breathable synthetic mesh, with an elasticized holster sewn to the side of the undershirt beneath each armhole. These are designed to be worn tight so that the gun does not flop around and, at Kramer's suggestion, I tightened mine by adding darts in the back and front.

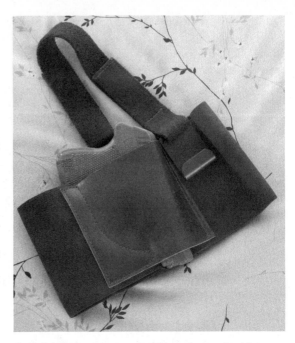

A thigh holster with a small, thin semi-auto pistol lets you wear pretty skirts and light summer blouses and still go armed.

Since Kramer's introduction of this concept, other manufacturers have extended it to the popular compression fabrics like the Under Armor brand, so there are several options that give you choices in the cut of the neckline, length of the holster undershirt, and more. Another application of the compression fabric technology is the compression shorts with an elasticized holster sewn over the buttocks area. The last is an option I've not personally tried.

Because the undershirt has to be put on by pulling it over the head, it is not practical to put the gun into the elasticized holster until you are wearing the garment. Starting with an unloaded

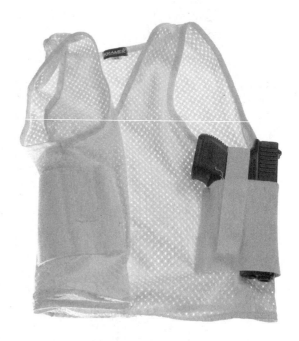

Undershirt holster with Glock Model 26.

Melissa demonstrates concealing a Glock Model 26 in the Kramer Undershirt holster by layering two shirts, a stretchy pull over topped by a fun printed bolero. This ensemble is particularly illustrative of the power of layers in concealment.

gun, you must work in front of a mirror or with a friend acting as safety observer to figure out how to pull open the elasticized holster and get your gun inside without pointing the muzzle of the gun toward your body or putting your fingers in front of the muzzle. It can be done, but requires great caution. I do not see how you will be able to reholster in this carry device after real-life use of the gun. Have another option worked out in advance.

In addition to undergarments, there is a wide array of trousers with holsters incorporated into the front pockets. These include CCW Breakaways and Blackie Collins' Toters Jeans. In addition, a number of the tactical clothiers add double layer pocket linings, zipable front pockets and other features that promote pocket carry. A lot of these are targeted at the men's market, but may be an option for some women, too.

Holster vests likewise are more often marketed toward men, though it would be entirely possible to alter a high-quality lined leather vest to mimic the only-briefly available women's leather carry vest from Coronado Leather that I have used for many years. The holster vest has been co-opted by the motorcycle riding clothing industry and you can find shapely leather vests for women that include holster pockets at online stores including Bikers' Den,[7] to identify only one.

Note the pullover's tendency to print the outline of the gun (ABOVE), *underscoring why we add another layer for concealment* (RIGHT).

Just like wearing a shoulder holster, the weight of a gun and magazines may weigh down on your trapezius muscles uncomfortably, so you may find yourself using carry vests for half a day or a quick errand only.

Kakadu Traders,[8] a company that makes an attractive line of canvas vests, jackets and cargo pants for both men and women, adds a layer of support fabric through the front and across the back of the shoulders to distribute the weight of guns and other items carried in the large front pockets. In addition, their jackets and vests feature very large front pockets with built-in holsters and the option to add a concealment shield to prevent the canvas from showing the gun's outline, since though it is a heavy fabric, the canvas is also quite soft.

Though casual, their concealment clothing line is attractively feminine, with A-line seams on the women's vest, and soft distressed canvas in a variety of colors from neutral grey, tan and muted green to a pale eggplant hue that gives their vest a feminine look. A soft leather collar dresses it up a little, too.

Concealed Carry Clothiers[9] has for many years sold a very well-equipped carry vest and they will sew their pattern up in the customer's fabric, too, giving you lots more op-

Kakadu Traders' women's vest is a prettier version of the standard canvas concealed carry vest. It has princess seams, a leather collar, and comes in a variety of colors including dusty rose and a nice mauve, eggplant color in addition to the olive hue pictured. In addition, the gun pockets are generously cut, so drawing is easier from this carry vest than from many other products on the market.

tions than always wearing one simple, tan or grey vest. The Concealment Shop in Mesquite, TX, has a fabric carry vest that is equipped with ambidextrous holster pockets[10] in a distressed canvas that is very good looking in a casual way.

Vests and trousers with holsters sewn in may prove safer for putting the gun in the holster without pointing at an arm or a leg, simply because they are looser than the undergarments that incorporate an elasticized pouch to hold a gun. If you use this type of holster clothing, start by working with a safety observer or in front of a mirror to be sure you aren't inadvertently pointing the muzzle at your leg, arm or body. Start out with plenty of practice with an un-loaded gun before using the holster clothing for concealed carry in public with a loaded gun.

HEIGHT AND WEIGHT

As with any concealed carry option, the size of the gun you carry must be a compromise between what is large enough for effective use in a life-and-death fight, and what you can conceal. Some of these non-holster options will only accommodate an extremely miniaturized handgun, especially when carried by women of petite build. Other concealment devices, owing to the location on which they are worn, will accept a slightly larger

Glock 26 is too big to effectively conceal under one layer of light or clingy fabric whether it is tucked under the arm or beneath the bosom. The options are to either go to a smaller, flatter gun like a KelTec P3AT in a smaller caliber, or add a sheer layer of camouflage to hide the blocky Glock 26. (TOP OF NEXT PAGE).

handgun, especially if you are willing to cover it with several layers of clothing or garments that look normal when worn slightly loose.

Purpose-built clothing has several drawbacks. First, it tends to be expensive. Then, for women, it imposes a lack of variety to the extent that your friends, coworkers and other associates may begin to ask why you always wear the same vest, nominate you for the TV show *What Not to Wear*, or offer to take you shopping so you can pick out a new jacket or pair of trousers. The concealment devices designed to be worn beneath regular clothing do not have this disadvantage and, while some are expensive, if one provides a means through which you can be armed as you go about your daily business, it can be well worth the initial cost.

(1) Galco International, ibid., Underwraps Belly Band, http://www.usgalco.com/HolsterPT3.asp?ProductID=2443&CatalogID=393

(2) Kathy Jackson, Cornered Cat Training Company, ibid.

(3) Smart Carry™, made by Concealed Protection 3, Inc., 940 7th Street NW, Largo, Florida 33770-1112, 888-459-2358, info@smartcarry.com http://www.smartcarry.com/

(4) Looper Law Enforcement Flashbang holster, 2124 S. Prospect Oklahoma City, OK 73129, 405-677-1655, customerservice@looperbrand.com http://flashbangholster.com/

(5) Galco International, ibid., Thigh Band holster, http://www.usgalco.com/HolsterPT3.asp?ProductID=2639&CatalogID=393

(6) Kramer Handgun Leather, ibid., Undershirt holster, http://www.kramerleather.com/products.cfm?categoryID=21

(7) The Bikers' Den, 2050 Beavercreek Rd, Suite 101 #104, Oregon City OR 97045, www.Bikersden.com

(8) Kakadu Traders Australia, Inc., 12832 NE Airport Way, Portland, OR 97230 800-852-5288 www.kakaduaustralia.com

(9) Concealed Carry Clothiers, LLC, P.O. Box 237, Saunderstown, RI 02879, 888-959-4500, http://concealedcarry.com/products/Women%27s-Hidden-Advantage-Vest.html

(10) The Concealment Shop, Inc., 15330 LBJ Freeway Suite 204, Mesquite, TX 75150, 800-444-7090, http://www.theconcealmentshop.com

GUN PURSES
AND PACKS

There are so many interesting holster packs and purses that we'll dedicate a chapter to these options. Holster waist packs are great, but do not always fit in, as would be the case in a dress worn to a church service. A holster purse, though, fits in to those circumstances very well, indeed. Off-body carry entails some considerable downsides, so we also need strategies to address these realistic concerns that arise when a gun is carried off-body in a holster handbag.

Matching your carry gear to your activity is one of the secrets to successful concealed carry. That usually requires at least two, if not three, concealment options, unless your activities are not very diverse. For example, your belt holster should work most of the time if you are able to dress primarily in trousers. Add a belly band, kangaroo pouch, thigh band holster or bra holster for use with skirts and dresses. These options should carry you through 99 percent of the activities in which you engage.

Some activities, especially recreational pursuits, are not well suited to using a more conventional holster. Participants in mountain biking, motorcycling or hiking commonly wear a waist pack of some kind to carry wallets, phones, cameras, lip balm and other personal items. For firearms, this concealment option was first adapted by DeSantis Gunhide, and their Gunny Sacks are still popular today [1]. These days a large number of manufacturers also make waist packs that contain holsters. These work very nicely in the recreational setting, except in the rare event that the waist pack, which is worn in the front over the abdomen, interferes with something like a saddle horn if horseback riding, or a tank bag if motorcycling, for example, though sometimes the pack can be shifted off center and will still work well.

Holster waist packs are usually comprised of two compartments, a large one at the back of the pack containing a rudimentary holster and security strap,

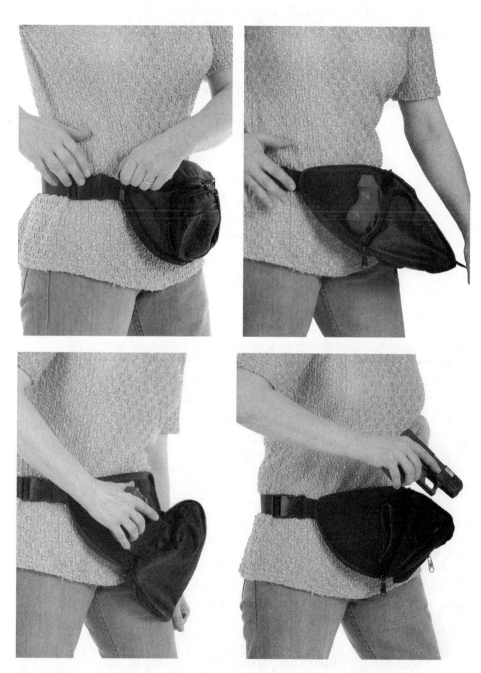

Drawing from the well-designed A.E. Pistol Pack [2] entails using the non-dominant hand to rip open the zipper, taking care to get the arm out of the muzzle's path before drawing the gun and attaining a two-handed shooting grip.

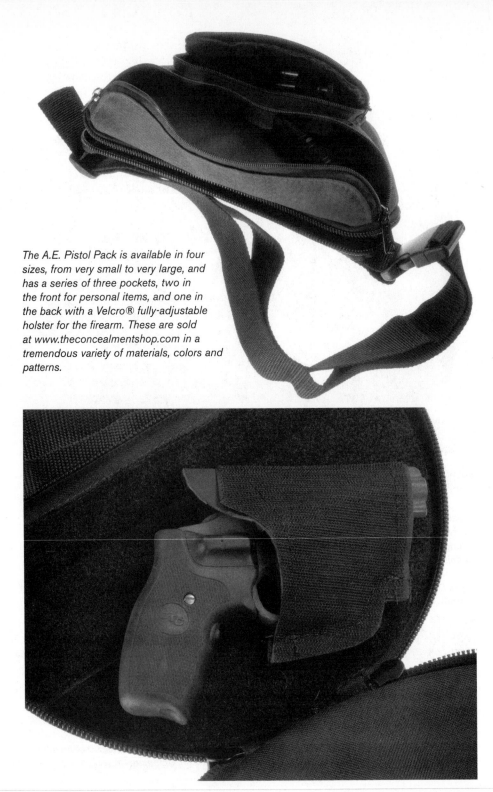

The A.E. Pistol Pack is available in four sizes, from very small to very large, and has a series of three pockets, two in the front for personal items, and one in the back with a Velcro® fully-adjustable holster for the firearm. These are sold at www.theconcealmentshop.com in a tremendous variety of materials, colors and patterns.

and occasionally an elastic loop in which to secure a spare magazine. A front compartment is set aside for your wallet, keys, phone and other personal items and this provides the camouflage to prevent people from thinking the pack contains a gun. Waist pack concealed carry is common and it may clue in other armed citizens, including law enforcement, that you are carrying a gun.

When legally carrying a gun, being identified by law enforcement or other armed citizens doesn't really deserve much worry. If, however, you worry that a waist pack is too recognizable and possibly provides a robber with "shoot me first" identification, then avoid leather waist packs and tan or black ballistic nylon pouches in favor of cheerful colors and funny prints. Borrow a "Nikon" logo off your camera bag so people think you are an amateur photographer, or sew on a logo patch from outdoors gear so you look like an avid hiker. Finally, only use the waist pack where those activities are normal.

Waist packs aren't appropriate to all styles of clothing. For example, a pack carried with most dresses is so incongruous that no one would think you were carrying anything but a gun pack. Reserve this method for casual clothing under circumstances where others use waist packs for hands-free carry of wallets, phones and other personal items.

Waist packs generally close with a heavy-duty zipper, though sometimes Velcro® is used. Since an ordinary zipper pull is small and can slip out of easy reach, many holster waist packs attach a lanyard to the zipper pull. An angled tug should open the pack enough that your dominant hand can access the grips of the gun. Take care before drawing that your non-dominant hand, the one pulling the zipper, is not still in front of the muzzle of the gun. Get in the habit of tugging so firmly on the front of the waist pack that if right-handed, you slam your left hand against the outside of your thigh at the end of the ripping motion. That gives you a tactile indicator that your non-gun hand is out of the way and it is safe to draw the gun.

Diane demonstrates the use of her A.E. Pistol Pack, to which she has added a slightly larger braided lanyard for easy use.

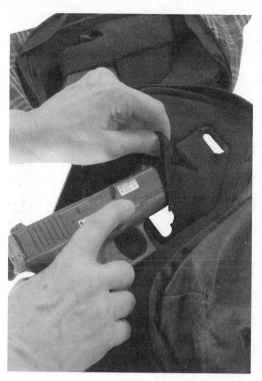

Returning the gun to a waist pack holster safely depends on the type of internal holster the device uses. Many waist packs contain a stiffened fabric holster into which it is entirely safe to slip the gun, taking care to keep your non-gun hand out of the path of the muzzle. Other waist packs use the very compact design of a stretchy neoprene panel into which a slot has been cut. The gun has to be slid through the slot where it is held snuggly against a thin plastic panel in the back. It is a wonderfully compact design, but not one into which you can expect to holster the gun rapidly, under stress, or by feel as would be required in the dark or while moving.

Before carrying in a waist pack, commit considerable time to dry fire drawing practice. Pitfalls include filling the front compartment so full that it binds up and

Waist pack with flat neoprene holsters make it very hard to get the gun safely into the holster without pointing at your fingers.

Coronado's pull-through holsters add safety to their waist packs. This distressed finish blends right in with motorcycle leathers and some other casual venues.

Roma Leathers [3] sells several models of holster handbags with a metallic cable sewn into the purse strap as theft prevention. Bags from Gun Tote'n Mamas [4] also have this added protection.

the closure won't unzip far enough to get a gun out. If the design lacks a security strap, the gun can fall out of some of the built in holsters when you rip open the zipper. Security straps should be designed so that a brisk tug on the gun disconnects the Velcro® or other closure without requiring an additional step to free the gun from the retention.

Waist packs have good security compared to other bags and packs, because they are worn strapped to your hips allowing you to keep your hands free. A waist strap that is reinforced with wire or mesh or other slash-proofing can provide an additional margin of safety, if you can find a holster pack that includes this safeguard. Finding this feature outside of the travel industry is not easy anymore, however, as it is not as common today as it was on early holster purses and gun packs. Some travel publications report that purse snatchers have began equipping themselves with wire cutters instead of knives or razors to slice through a purse or pack strap. You will need to decide what level of security makes sense for the circumstances under which you will be using a holster pack or bag to carry and conceal a handgun.

Gun Tote'n Mamas put a lot of effort into creating holster handbags with attractive features ladies would want to carry even without a gun inside, as is certainly true for the attractive but low-key "Simple Bling!" model shown here.

IN THE BAG

The variety of holster handbags marketed to armed women is nearly endless. The strongest argument in favor of carrying a handgun in a holster purse is the freedom it provides to always carry your gun, regardless of the style of clothing required by the circumstances into which you are going, so long as you can carry a purse. In addition, because women's purses are often large and capacious, they accommodate a full-sized, fully equipped handgun. This is a great answer to the problematic trend by concealed carry practitioners to carry such a miniaturized handgun that critical elements like a slide lock are deleted to trim size, or the caliber of ammunition it fires is subpar for defense against an aggressive, determined attacker. Those are two strong arguments in favor of holster handbags.

Naturally, were we to attempt to review specific holster handbags our information would be outdated before we were done. Suffice it to say that there is no shortage of attractive, stylish bags ranging from quite small clutches to very large totes, in leather or fabric, some with attractive buckles, snaps and other "bling," some with long straps for cross-body carry, regular or adjustable shoulder straps, and a myriad of other features that blend the bag's function between handbag and holster bag.

Avoid designs that do not put a layer of cushioning between the gun and the outer panel so that through daily use, the outline of the gun does not become imprinted and visible on the side of the bag.

While a few of the gun purses marketed look a little plain or might strike you as a little outdated if you are avidly fashion-conscious, the colors, shapes and ornamentation offered by many holster purse manufacturers are extraordinarily fashionable. Some will object bitterly when asked to pay between $200 or $300 for a high-end holster handbag. Before you complain, do an Internet search on "designer handbag" and compare prices for mere fashion handbags.

What sets a holster bag apart from an ordinary purse is a separate compartment that is reserved exclusively for your handgun. This protects your privacy so your gun is not visible when you reach for your phone or wallet. More important, though, is the safety the separate compartment provides, protecting the gun from becoming entangled all the other stuff that occupies a purse. Carrying a gun is a serious undertaking, and requires more attention to safety than just dropping the gun into a purse with the rest of your belongings.

The gun compartments are fastened through a variety of methods, using zippers, strips of Velcro® or snaps. While the greatest shopping variety can be found on the Internet, buying online does not give you a way to test the closure to see if it faces the right direction for your most efficient draw stroke, if you can smoothly operate the zipper or Velcro®, or if the opening into the holster compartment is large enough for your gun.

Many years ago, I remember teaching an optional session on holster handbags that I occasionally offered upon request when teaching women's handgun classes. I was surprised at one session when a woman bitterly complained that the only gun purse she liked in the selection I provided for the ladies to try used Velcro® closures that abraded her hands when she reached inside the compartment to draw the gun. It was a feature that would have kept her from practicing drawing from the bag, and thus was too great of a disadvantage to make the bag of much use to her. The experience illustrated the need for hands-on experience with an expensive purchase like a holster handbag, or at least the need for a fault-free return policy if you buy from the manufacturer's website.

Most holster handbags incorporate a vertical opening on one side of the bag to access a separate gun compartment at the back or in the center of the bag. A few holster bags open from the top, a design I personally favor because this carries the gun oriented similarly to the belt holsters from which most formal training teaches drawing and presenting a handgun. A top opening is also ambidextrous, and that is very important, in light of possibilities that you may be operating one handed if you are holding a child or if one hand or arm is injured in a fight leading up to needing the gun.

Some sellers will tell you that any gun purse is ambidextrous, but I'm skeptical of that claim. Most bag designs have an obvious front, usually indicated by

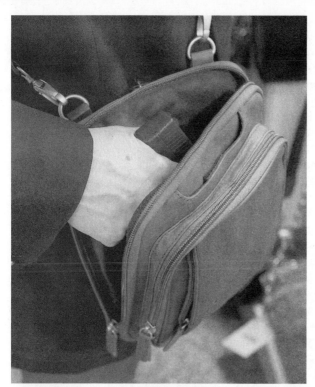

Drawing from Gun Tote'n Mamas vertical carry, top access bag is much like drawing from an appendix carry belt holster, just lower. Author prefers this orientation over bags that open for a horizontal draw stroke.

small pockets, a flap over the opening, attractive metallic buckles or other design elements with a plain back on the opposite side of the bag. Whether you carry the ornamented side to the outside of your body will depend on how you orient the opening to the holster compartment. That opening must face forward when you carry the bag on your non-dominant side shoulder and being right-handed or left-handed determines how it must be carried.

Getting a gun out of a holster handbag generally takes about twice as long as drawing from a belt holster.[5] If you need to carry in a holster handbag, you must find ways to mitigate this speed disadvantage. In a high-risk area like a dark parking garage, that may mean walking with your hand on the grips of the gun while it is still in the bag's holster compartment. To avoid looking odd, you can drape a jacket or shawl over the bag to conceal your hand inside your purse. This is another reason you need to be able to inspect a holster purse in detail before buying, since the size and orientation of the opening has a big influence on how difficult it is to draw the gun. If the bag you are considering requires two hands to access and draw the gun, pass on it, since you may only have one hand with which to do the job.

These are disadvantages to carrying a self-defense gun in a handbag, but there is an even worse downside. Your purse is rarely attached to your person at all times. When you set your purse down, or if your purse is forcibly taken from you, you lose not just your purse, but also the handgun for which you are responsible. When a purse-snatcher steals and runs away with just a purse, most women recognize that it is less dangerous to let him go, while they rush to a phone to cancel all those credit cards! A woman carrying a holster handbag is more inclined to fight over the bag and may be injured in the attempt to retain her gun purse.

I enjoyed a spirited discussion about holster handbags and security with long-time defensive shooting trainer, Vicki Farnam[6], who believes that concealed carry using a holster handbag is an extremely viable option for women. If targeted for purse snatching, she explains that she would fight to keep her handbag, whether it held a gun or not, to avoid losing credit cards, identification containing her home address, and other personal details. Asked about the common advice to never get into a scuffle with a purse snatcher, she looked at me in amazement, since blandly accepting criminal victimization simply is not in her mindset. "Never is an awful long time," she warned. "What is in my purse is not worth my life, but it might be worth getting banged up over. Someone could grab a gun out of your belt holster, too. It is not a perfect world," she reminded me. "I'm always worried about keeping track of my handbag, because whether there is a gun in it or not, I keep other things in there that also need to be secured. It is always over my shoulder. I don't set it down, and I don't leave it in the basket while shopping. If I set it down at the office, I find a place where I can keep contact with it, but no one else can have contact with it."

She explains that the gun holstered in a purse gives a margin of safety when using the restroom, since a purse goes with you into the stall and with no need to take special steps to secure it, no gun handling occurs in the public restroom, Vicki explains. "You don't have to worry about your belt, your holster or

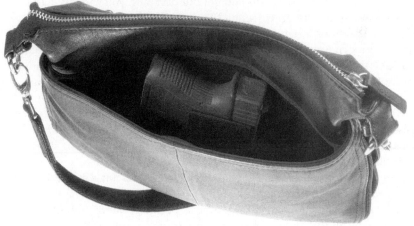

Another Gun Tote'n Mamas bag opens from the top, the left side and the right side, so the armed woman can set up the interior holster to accommodate her preferred access to the gun.

your gun, when you have to undo your pants."

A more prevalent danger is simply setting the bag down where a thief finds it easy to pick up and carry away. If you carry a gun in a purse, it must remain on your lap or tightly snugged between both feet at restaurants and other venues. Vicki explained that in crowded environments where she needed both hands free, she will sling the bag cross body, where it is held closer to her side for greater security.

For casual activities like hiking or attending an all-day conference, she likes a smaller approximately 6"x9" bag in which the holster holds the gun vertically, much as a belt holster does. By moving the bag strap off her left shoulder to the right, but slinging the bag cross body, she can keep the holster in approximately the same position, while giving her shoulders a break from the weight.

When visiting friends or at a party, maintaining control of a holster handbag is not so easily accomplished. Some bags have locking zippers, and engaging the lock is a partial solution, though a determined child or a thief will only be slowed, not stopped, by such precautions and, of course, leaving it locked all the time makes the gun too inaccessible to expect to grab it fast enough for self defense.

We must never allow a gun carried in a purse to be treated with careless indifference. Several years ago a woman's granddaughter accessed her gun while the child and the handbag were in a shopping cart at a large discount department store. I am sure the grandmother never imagined that the toddler would dredge around in her purse, and certainly could not conceive that the child would pull out and fire her handgun, but that is what happened. The child underwent surgery after shooting herself and survived, but things could have ended far more tragically. This lesson emphasizes the need for extreme vigilance when carrying a handgun in a purse. If you cannot keep the purse secured, please do not carry a gun in it.

If targeted for victimization while you are in your car, will you remember to grab your holster handbag if you decide that your best tactic is to flee on foot? If you are involved in an accident from which you need to get out of the car to interact with other drivers, will you get out carrying your holster handbag positioned where you can draw from it? Few people would. These are serious drawbacks to carrying a handgun off-body.

If you are driving with a purse-holstered handgun, find a way to secure the bag through the seat belt or between your thigh and the car door or in a deep pocket built into the door, so that if an attack is initiated by causing your car to crash, your gun and purse are not flung beyond reach or where you may not be able to find it in the confusion. This happened to FBI Agent John Hanlon when a revolver lodged beneath his leg went flying to the floor when the car he was in crashed as they arrived at the scene of the infamous FBI shootout with killers Platt and Matix in Miami, FL, in 1986.

There are definite disadvantages to purse carry. It is not a method that I have needed to use extensively. Still, were my circumstances to change, I would continue to carry a gun as much of the time as possible, and if that meant carrying in a holster handbag, I would not hesitate to do so. I would take considerable caution to buffer against the dangers unique to concealed carry in a purse with extra precautions like those we've talked about here. As Vicki Farnam encourages, "It seems to me that we shouldn't eliminate purse or off-body carry just because we think there is some necessity of putting a purse down and that we would forget about it. If your mind is already set that, 'OK, I am carrying a gun,' and you say that to yourself every morning when you get ready and you leave home, 'I am carrying a gun today,' well, then every time you use the restroom, you are thinking about your gun, or every time you walk into an office or into a store or in to somebody's home, and then you turn around and leave at some later time, you ask, 'OK, do I have everything? Yes.' "

"I have heard women say over and over again, 'I would never carry in a handbag. I would never do off-body carry.' Well, never is a long time! Why are we not flexible? It is not as easy for women to carry consistently in one fashion as it is for men. We can look at this philosophy in one of two ways," she urges. "One: I will always make sure that my wardrobe accommodates concealing a gun. Or, for other women, they look at it a different way, and they say, 'I will find a way to conceal a gun and dress the way I prefer to dress in my fashion style.' "

If your circumstances dictate carrying a handgun in a holster handbag, you must take extra care to do so safely. That includes keeping the bag secured when it is not in your possession, and carrying the bag with you at times when you might set an ordinary handbag down and step away from it. Still, it can be done, and consistently carrying a personal protection handgun—yes, in a holster hand-bag—is advantageous. As Vicki Farnam concludes, "We hear this philosophy all the time that it is not good practice to carry off body. Well, I just disagree with that, because women who are used to carrying purses are used to taking care of their purses. As women started to carry, men said, 'You need to carry on your waistline,' because that is where men carried guns. Well, that is not the best place in the world if a women has a small child she has to pick up all the time. It is not the best place to carry if there is no way for you to conceal it, or if you don't have a secure holster or if the gun that you have chosen is very big and bulky, then it is not necessarily the best place."

If you use a holster handbag as one of your concealed carry options, you must add practice time to be sure you are able to draw safely and as quickly as possible from the holster handbag. Use dry fire practice to hone drawing an unloaded gun from waist packs, purses and other carry packs until bringing the gun on target is safe, fast and smooth. Use a mirror, a laser sight or have a companion watch and give feedback to make sure the non-dominant hand and arm are never in front of the muzzle.

(1) DeSantis Gunhide, Gunny Sack, http://www.desantisholster.com/store/SEARCH-BY-HOLSTER-OR-ACCESSORY/GUNNY-SACKS--GUN-CADDIES

(2) A.E. Pistol Packs from The Concealment Shop, Inc., 15330 LBJ Freeway Suite 204, Mesquite, TX 75150, 972-289-8997, http://www.theconcealmentshop.com/aepacks.php

(3) Roma Leathers, 1180 E Francis St., Bldg. B, Ontario, CA 91761, 800-998-7662, http://www.roma-gunbags.com/

(4) Gun Tote'n Mamas, Concealed Carry Handbags by Gun Tote'n Mamas , 1303 Shermer Road , Northbrook, IL 60062, 847-446-0700 Ext. 204, https://www.guntotenmamas.com, gtm@guntotenmamas.com

(5) Kathy Jackson in SWAT Magazine http://www.swatmag.com/issues/view/january_2012

(6) Vicki Farnam, Defense Training International, P.O. Box 917, LaPorte, CO, 80535, 970-482-2520, http://www.defense-training.com

THE PLIGHT OF
THE LEFT-HANDED
SHOOTER

Scientific studies estimate that over 10 percent of the population is left handed, and the incidences of left handedness run a little higher among the female population. Since not all armed citizens are right handed, it makes sense to talk to the left-handed reader for a few pages. Right-handed readers can also learn from this chapter, since we are all only one injury accident away from having to adapt to limits on full use of our dominant hands and arms.

It is a right-handed world. That's a fact left-handed readers don't need me to point out. Scissors, handguns, can openers, rifles, pruning shears and many more tools are designed to work for and are marketed for right-handed consumers. A lot of holsters are subject to the same bias, with designers and manufacturers estimating that 87 percent of potential customers will be right handed. A small manufacturer interested in maximizing sales for the minimum investment of time and effort will inevitably make holsters for right-handed shooters. Likewise, a retail gun store has to decide how many—if any—left-side holsters it is practical for them to stock, knowing that they will not sell as quickly, if they sell at all.

Fortunately, it is a lot easier to buy guns that function well for lefties, since a lot of modern guns work just fine for left-handed shooters, though sometimes a few of the operational steps need to be modified. For example, the cylinder release on the standard double-action revolver is positioned where it falls naturally beneath the thumb when gripped by a right-handed shooter. The lefty must adapt reloading technique around that disadvantage, but beyond that, reloading the revolver left handed is in some ways smoother than it is for the right handed shooter.

With the semi-auto, often the magazine release is designed so that the release button can be switched to the right side of the gun, where it can be employed with the shooting-hand thumb as is normally taught. On other designs, a magazine release button or lever is accessible from either side, as is done on

Practicing left-handed revolver reloads starts by pressing the cylinder release latch with the left thumb (TOP LEFT) as the right hand moves up to push the cylinder through the frame window with the thumb coming through to hold the cylinder and keep it from turning. (TOP RIGHT)The right hand, now supporting the revolver by the cylinder, inverts the gun, muzzle up, and the heel of the right hand gives the ejector rod a brisk slap (MIDDLE LEFT) ejecting the empty cases. Next, point the muzzle straight down, as the left hand brings the speed loader to the cylinder. (BOTTOM LEFT) Drop the empty speed loader as soon as it releases the cartridges, (BOTTOM RIGHT) and close the cylinder as you orient the gun back toward the target and re-attain your two-handed shooting grip.

the Walther P99. Absent that accommodation, though, learn to release the magazine with the left index finger, which with good hand flexibility may actually be faster than the traditional right-handed magazine release method.

Most semi-automatic handguns are equipped with a slide lock/release lever located on the left side of the gun (with the exception of certain Heckler & Koch models and FN Herstal model FNS™9). With most semi-automatic handguns, when locking the action open or clearing a double feed, the right-handed shooter manipulates the slide lock with the right-hand thumb. For the lefty, of course, the lever is on the wrong side, so she learns to grip the slide in her right hand to both withdraw it and to reach over and pull up on the slide lock lever. It takes a little practice, and care must be taken not to cover the ejection port with the palm of the hand until the gun is unloaded, but once learned this technique is entirely functional.

Left-handed operation of the semi-automatic pistol slide lock starts with several brisk racks of the slide to be sure the chamber is empty, then slipping the right hand over the top of the slide so the thumb can engage the slide lock.

It's easy to release the magazine with the left hand trigger finger if the gun has not been custom fit with a right-side magazine release for the left-handed shooter. Once learned, this magazine release method is fast! The author knows a right-handed shooting champion who refit her competition guns with right-side magazine releases so she could release the magazine with her trigger finger.

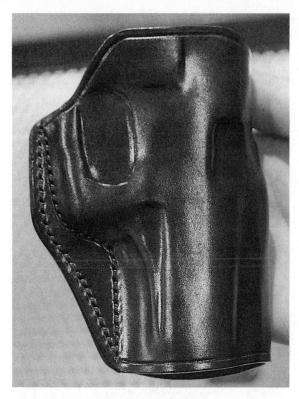

You liked what you saw of Galco's Stinger holster when you checked out the right-handed model in the gun store. Now, can you find one for left-side carry?

Left-handed shooters need holsters that are oriented correctly when worn on the left side. Buying from larger holster manufacturers increases chances of finding gear for left-handed shooters. Buying off the Internet increases chances of finding left-side holsters, since many of these sales are fulfilled through a drop shipping arrangement by which the retailer does not have to hold the stock in inventory. Let us say that you have settled on, for example, Galco's Stinger holster as an affordable first belt holster. You know from Internet research that it is made for a variety of handgun models including yours and, hallelujah, it has the option of left handed models! You are ecstatic until, to your frustration, you can find examples of the Stinger holster in several of your local gun shops, but none for your model of gun or in the left-handed variation.

Use the stock on hand in your retail gun store to assure yourself of the quality of construction, and that you like the orientation of the holster on your belt. Ask the retailer if they make special orders. They may ask for a deposit against the purchase, to avoid being stuck with a holster they cannot sell if the customer does not return to make the purchase when the holster arrives from their supplier. If you have a gun shop in which the clerks treat you with respect and care, you really should support them by giving them your trade. Otherwise, when you go back, their doors may be locked and an "Out of Business" sign posted in the window.

Then again, you may choose to go online and search until you find an online retailer selling the exact holster that you need. A large Internet retail website usually employs search algorithms that will bring up pages upon pages of products that have left-handed options available. It may take some diligent browsing to find exactly what you really need and want, but using this resource is considerably better than conditions were in the pre-Internet era when the left-handed shooter endured much greater difficulty pulling together all the concealment gear they needed. Given the ubiquity of the Internet these days, putting together a full set of left-side gear is much easier than it once was.

Magazine pouches may or may not be ambidextrous, depending on how accurately they are molded to the magazine they are intended to carry. Traditional technique carries magazines with the bullet tips facing forward, based on thinking that it is strongest to twist the hand around to orient the magazine the proper direction to feed the magazine into the gun and seat it firmly using the palm of the hand against the base plate. In addition, this orientation allows the

After putting the magazine in the gun, the left-handed shooter racks the slide and releases it briskly, after pulling it back as far as it will go. If the hand moves forward as the gun's recoil spring sends the slide into battery, she may cause a malfunction by deterring the force it needs to pick up a cartridge of ammunition off the top of the magazine and feed it into the chamber then lock up the slide and barrel in preparation to safely fire.

index finger to "point" the magazine into the magazine well, and that helps during reloads while moving or in the dark.

Alternatively, I have known several accomplished shooters who, opposite to that conventional wisdom, carried their magazines backwards. They explained that they found it slower to twist the hand around to get the magazine oriented correctly to load into the gun. If stuck with magazine pouches designed to be carried on the right side, the left handed shooter may wish to try this reload

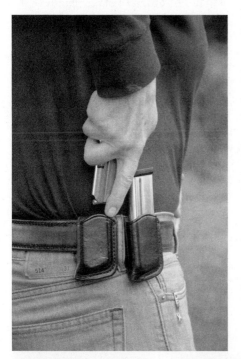

If stuck with right-handed magazine pouches, the left handed shooter might choose to modify the reloading technique to accommodate bullets pointing backward on the left side. While those trained in the classic bullets-forward reload may find this disturbing, with practice, it can become just as natural.

method. Otherwise, reserve your business for manufacturers who make products for left-handed shooters, or patronize a custom leatherworker.

Once you have been carrying for a year or so, have received some quality training, and have developed solid ideas about how you want to conceal your self-defense gun, it may be time to go to a custom holster maker and specify exactly the type of holster that you want. Specify that you want one that you can carry on your left side, plus aspects like holster angle, how high or low it sits on your belt, whether it is worn inside the waistband or out, and other details that ease the inconvenience and discomfort of going armed. Ask the holster maker how they will deal with requests for adjustments, and do your best to be very specific about what you want and need so you will not find yourself wishing you could return an expensive, custom-made holster. Returns of custom holsters, I predict, may be about as welcome as returning an expensive dress that you've had custom tailored in an unusual color or fabric.

Though the left-handed shooter may feel that the whole world is against her, there are a reasonable number of manufacturers and crafts people making and selling holsters out of small shops who are happy to make left-side holsters and related gear for the lefty's carry and use. Take advantage of these, since trying to adapt a holster made specifically for right-side carry is rarely satisfactory.

DRESSING
AROUND THE GUN

Is your skirt and high-heels fashion not an option if you carry a gun? Does the armed woman face times when fashion expectations mean she will not be able to carry a gun? What clothing compromises will you need to make to consistently carry a concealed handgun? Casual, work fashions, dress-up and more…we'll look at how women maintain their own personal fashion sense and still carry guns for their own defense.

Regularly carrying a gun for personal protection will require changes to your wardrobe unless you default to carrying in a holster handbag. To tell a woman otherwise is disingenuous, and risks failures from which she may conclude that she really cannot pull this off. Nothing could be further from the truth! Still, compromises will be required, and if we start with that as our working premise, we will find that looking pretty and carrying a handgun for personal protection are not mutually exclusive.

When using an inside-the-waistband holster for best concealability, there is no way to avoid needing an inch or two more ease in trouser waistband measurements to accommodate the bulk of the gun and holster. Depending on how snug current women's fashions are (and these days fashionable clothing is very tight indeed), buying a larger waist size may make another measurement like hip or thigh disproportionate, causing the trousers to look baggy and sloppy. Consider tailoring or home alterations to take in seams to reduce extra fabric across the hips or other areas that don't need the extra room to accommodate a gun. For denim jeans and casual trousers, some have found that buying men's jeans avoids the tightly contoured waistline in women's wear that really will not accommodate your handgun and an IWB holster. The men's Levi®'s can fit snuggly in the posterior while giving an inch or so of ease in the waistband for an IWB-holstered gun.

You may also need to consider tailoring to modify the cut of suit jackets if your job entails a dressy, executive work environment. With blazers and jackets, we face concerns about sufficient looseness around the waist or torso, depend-

Figure 1

Figure 2

Figure 3

Figure 4

Figure 5   Figure 6

FIGURES 1-5: *Kathy's pretty print jersey dress is feminine and attractive. Until she draws the KelTec P3AT from the Flashbang Marilyn holster under her left arm, there is no hint that she is armed. Even without the camouflaging bolero, the Marilyn holster is quite invisible when the dress is simply worn sleeveless!* (FIGURE 6)

ing on where you are carrying the gun. When blazers and jackets are figure-hugging and tucked in at the waist, they make belt holsters and guns in belly bands harder to conceal. When this profile is in vogue, you may find yourself moving the belly band up your torso and putting the gun below your armpit or bust line. If providing coverage for the extra bulk of the gun means buying a larger size, you may need the services of a tailor or a skilled seamstress to tuck in the waistline and make blouses, jackets and blazers fit properly at the shoulders while leaving enough fullness in the body to hide a holstered gun.

MIX IT UP

As noted in earlier chapters, women who carry a concealed handgun daily often find that having only one holster just doesn't work because women's clothing choices are terribly specific to the activity in which we are engaged. Athletic clothing is even specific to the sport for which it is worn, so to say that a waist pack will work when you are part of a recreational activity is an oversimplification. We will succeed better by categorizing types of clothing, and identifying carry methods that may work with these styles.

Here are some examples--

1. Trousers: The design needs a waistband and belt loops; the fabric must be sturdy; and the fit should be snug to body. These are optimum conditions for carrying in an IWB holster or belt scabbard, or if covered by a blazer or a loose, long and untucked shirt or jacket, an OWB belt scabbard. If the trouser legs are roomy and the pant legs are worn long, an ankle holster may work to conceal a small handgun.

2. Skirt or trousers without a waistband or functional belt loops: If the fit over waist and hips is snug, try concealing in a bellyband, bra-holster or Kramer Undershirt, and add a looser over-garment to the ensemble to hide the bulge of the gun. If the garment is somewhat gathered or pleated below the waist or worn baggy, concealing a small, flat handgun in a SmartCarry™ pouch or a bellyband may work

Example 1. Trousers

Example 2. Skirt or trousers without a waistband or functional belt loops

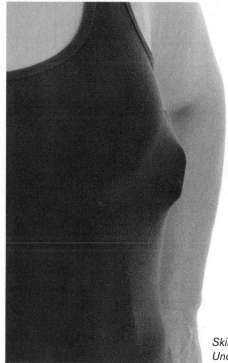

Skinny jeans, low cut tank top over Kramer Undershirt cannot hide the gun until the outfit is topped with the fun bolero. (Example 3)

3. Entire outfit has skin-hugging fit, as with leggings and a body hugging tank top, for example. Use a bellyband, Kramer Undershirt or compression wear with built in holsters, then layer a light blouse or vest, or maybe use several layers of blouses and vests for camouflage if the clothing is lacey, crocheted or semi-sheer.

One of the most important compromises you must achieve is between situation-appropriate clothing and a gun that is big enough for defensive use. For example, it would be silly to strap a holster waist pack over a pretty floral dress worn to church and consider that an effective means of concealing a handgun. Work environments in particular can set rigid wardrobe standards, but an unstated expectation on how you must dress may be a factor in certain social situations, too, and how we carry a gun must factor in these unwritten "dress codes." Take heart, though, we generally have more options than we usually think. We only need to start thinking creatively.

First, whenever possible, put together fashionable ensembles comprised of multiple layers. Though we use the word "concealment," I believe it is misleading. The term we ought to use is camouflage, and nothing camouflages odd gun-shaped bulges as well as two or three layers!

What needs to be camouflaged? The sharp angles and the outline of the grips and sometimes the barrel, depending on type of holster used and carry position. As in nature, straight lines and sharp angles draw the eye, since they are not consistent with the body's organic curves. Some camouflage depends on carry methods that blend the angles of the gun so it is hidden against the bulk of your body. For example, instead of allowing a handgun's grips to protrude beyond the line of the torso, be sure to carry the gun at an angle that puts body mass behind grips, muzzle and other recognizable gun elements. Once all we

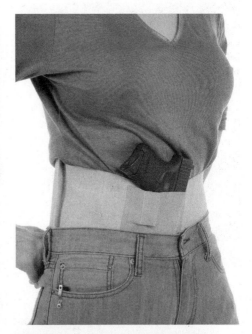

Location, location, location! Bellybands let us move the gun around to find its most concealable position. That certainly is not right on the point of the hip where grips stick out beyond the lines of the torso (ABOVE LEFT). . . *compared to the same Glock 26 and bellyband moved forward so the pistol's grips camouflage beneath the bosom when worn beneath the pullover with an over-garment added* (ABOVE RIGHT) . . . *or behind the hip where it hides against the ribcage and under a light layer of camouflage.* (RIGHT)

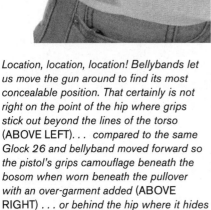
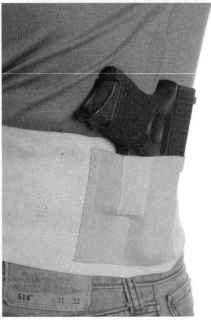

need to hide is the general lump created by the handgun, we can move on to more refined concealment/camouflage methods.

Multiple layers represent a time-proven concealment technique. This does not necessarily mean always wearing bulky sweaters and thick jackets in which you become overheated. Practiced artfully, the topmost camouflage layer can be quite light or even semi-sheer if you wear another light layer between it and the gun. Examples include blouse sets comprised of a solid colored sleeveless top covering the handgun. Alone, the base layer would offer poor concealment indeed because the gun's outline would easily show through. Cover the base layer with a color-coordinated open-fronted blouse, perhaps a loose, gathered velvet burnout pullover with a banded bottom or a pretty print semi-sheer linen peasant shirt.

Another method that works well for some is a slim camisole worn as the base layer beneath a loose sleeveless top with generous gathering at either the neckline or at an empire waistline. All that gathered fabric conceals like magic, especially if the gun is carried forward of the hip where the fabric drapes the most fully. These fashions include multi-tiered designs, and draped or cowl-fronted pullovers. The profusion of cloth provides plenty of camouflage for a holstered gun. Paired with skinny jeans, leggings or a pencil skirt, all those frilly, bouncy, ruffled layers draw attention away from the torso where the gun is hidden.

Alternatively, a crisply starched blouse or jacket can cover a holstered handgun without draping so clingingly that the outline of the gun prints through, because the starch gives the fabric stiffness. This is particularly important if carrying at or behind the hip, where the clothing tends to drape straight from the shoulder, is less likely to be generously gathered, and where the way we sit, bend and move pulls the covering fabric a little tighter over a behind-the-hip holstered handgun. In addition to a crisply starched finish, fabrics with an uneven texture, like coarsely woven tapestry, corduroy or an intentionally crinkled surface, for example, are less likely to cling to the outline of the gun and reveal its presence. Finally, bold prints and patterns distract the eye from the outline of the gun.

A bold printed pattern is easier to integrate in a casual wardrobe. Look for shirts, jackets and vests in southwestern or tribal prints or a fun leopard or zebra pattern. There is always the classic floral pattern rendered boldly, or a geometric or abstract print and even paisley! Stripes or plaids or tweeds may also work, though you will need to experiment to find out how small the pattern can be and still break up the outline of the gun, since when rendered in miniature, a tiny pattern essentially looks like a solid, as can be true for herringbone and a very small hounds tooth weave.

If concealing a belt-holstered handgun, the variety of blouses, tops, jackets and vests useful for concealment is nearly endless. For the most part, you will want the over-garment to extend below the bottom of your belt by perhaps an inch or two if carrying in an IWB holster. That is the safest. However, with a tuckable holster camouflaged by an extra clothing layer you can get away with a shorter jacket or shirt, though I have always struggled with what to do with my spare magazines when the gun and holster were hidden in a tuckable holster beneath a shirt.

For shoulder holsters, cropped shirts and jackets, like pretty little boleros cut on a boxy profile and worn a little loose, hide a handgun so long as parts of the harness or clips do not show below the hem or above the neckline. Kramer's Undershirt holster positions the gun in a similar location and with it, all you need to worry about is that the neckline of your blouse is a little higher than the Under-shirt's neckline, which is cut like a tank top, so should not peek out from all but the most low-cut necklines. If you wear skin-tight fashions, cover the Undershirt first with a tight, clingy shirt, and then cam-ouflage the inevitable print of your gun's outline with a bo-lero or one of the larger sweater shrugs that is knit, crocheted, or made of velvet, slubbed silk

Muzzle end of shoulder holster prints badly through the small hound's-tooth pattern of this blazer.

or other fun fabric, like, perhaps a quilted patchwork or an embroidered ethnic design, as we have demonstrated several times already in this book.

Some boleros are cut more like sweater shrugs, and these, of course, aren't large enough to offer much concealment. In addition to proper cut, fabrics are important, though even heavily ruffled chiffon or something exotic like a se-quined or feathered bolero can provide amazing concealment for a small hand-gun for fancy dress parties. Who would ever suspect that a woman in a party gown topped with the dramatic feather or sequined bolero is concealing a gun?

One would think that the classic sweater set would work for layered con-cealment, but in single knit fabrics, I've had little luck eliminating the outline printed through both layers even if the outside sweater is quite lose, owing to the thinness of the knitted fabrics and the solid colors prevalent in this fashion.

Distraction is a key principle present in effective camouflage. If color and pattern in the fabric leave a little of the gun's bulge apparent, an eye-catching necklace, scarf, flamboyant hat or fun-loving hair style can pull the eye up from the belt line until a little printing will go largely unnoticed. Despite the gun's obvious and unforgettable weight on your body, most of the people around you are so self-involved that a little extra bulk on your right hip or your left ribcage does not even register in their consciousness.

Fashionable vests, boleros or jackets come in the guise of the fashion statements that a lot of women add atop sheer blouses, low cut necklines and skin-tight pullovers. Modesty layers work great when we need to camouflage a small handgun carried in a bellyband, a Kramer Undershirt or a shoulder holster. Longer vests and ruffled open-fronted jackets may do the same for the belt-holstered handgun.

Concealment potential of many garments is usually apparent in the store, but it makes the best sense to go to the clothing store wearing your concealed, holstered gun, not only for your own safety in the shopping center, but so you can be sure your new clothing purchases provide the concealment you hope they will. So, for example, though I carry in a belt holster 99 percent of the time, if I've decided that dressing for an impending wedding may call for a form-fitting sheath dress covered by a short lacy bolero or jacket, I can save myself a lot of hassle if I just show up at the fitting room wearing the gun and the Kramer Undershirt holster that I hope to use with the outfit, then plead modesty or other embarrassment to keep at bay helpful clerks outside the fitting room. When possible, it can help to take a sympathetic friend who knows you carry a gun to the store with you and she can run interference.

In fitting rooms and while shopping, to ensure maximum safety leave the gun in its holster and limit your gun handling to only what is entirely unavoidable. Do not take the gun in and out of its holster inside a dressing room where, especially if in a multi-floor department store, there literally is no safe direction in which to point the gun.

For most armed women, the key is working out wardrobe compromises that will conceal a reasonably accessible handgun without having to dress like a man. If there is one plea for help that resonates with armed women, it is, "How can I carry a defensive handgun and still dress like a woman?" In recent years, a plethora of websites for armed women have blossomed, joining the cornerstone armed women's educational website, www.corneredcat.com. Since being somewhat shortsighted in focusing on the "I can't" aspect of any difficult problem is a very human shortcoming, you may find it very helpful to read about a variety of solutions implemented by a number of women, gleaning those most applicable to yourself. Discussion with other armed women is also helpful, and online shooter's forums often reserve sections exclusively for women in which you can post anonymously. If your state's rifle and pistol association has a website or chat forum, check into it to see if they have a women's section set aside on which you can post questions that other female armed citizens may be able to help with, or simply encourage you woman-to-woman.

The online community, as well as female friends you make at the shooting range and classes, can all provide ideas that you can convert to fit into your own concealment and camouflage needs.

CHANGING SITUATIONS

The more things change…the more they stay the same. For the armed citizen, this is another way of saying that although we go through many life phases, the need for self defense is continuous. This chapter is about how armed women adapt to differing fashions, how changes in jobs, having children, life style and other ups and downs influence choices we make about carrying and possessing defensive weapons.

Youth and beauty–what more could a woman ask? Still, I really do not envy young women because most shoulder a much heavier burden of fashion consciousness, at a time when dressing smartly and fitting in with peers is extremely important. And young women's fashions are form-fitting, skin-baring, and attention-attracting. Add to that the social aspect of the young singles scene, be that sports, parties, and the unpredictability of those first few years living out from under the thumb of Mom and Dad. This time of exploration is rife with opportunities for victimization and violence, so it is only reasonable that sensible young women should find a handgun carried concealed an appropriate means of buffering all the dangers inherent in this footloose period of life.

This is the time of life when the young female is driven to draw attention. Overcoming Ol' Mother Nature is a pretty tall order, so it is unreasonable to tell young women to change too much. It is entirely possible to blend the protections enjoyed by the armed citizen with the 20-something life style, though imagination and compromise is required. For this age group, many of the camouflage methods we discussed in the last chapter will support concealed carry. When fashions are skin-baring, choose one area you will cover, whether that is your waistline, immediately below the bust line or the inside upper thigh, for example, and carry a concealed handgun there. Use fashion features like costume jewelry, scarves, hats or belts to draw the eye away from where the gun is carried.

Of course, those principles work for women of any age. Young women, living away from home for the first time, do need to learn the value of privacy, especially where self-defense weapons are concerned. Friends who fill the need to confide secrets formerly met by family are not good confidants for extremely private details like gun ownership. Young adults form intimate bonds with great ease, and it is common to tell too much too early, only to find the friendship dissolving and with it any promises to protect your secrets. Keep your self-defense guns secret. Protecting your privacy requires more effort, but for best success, you must not tell.

Shared housing is common with this age group. This makes secure gun storage mandatory. A sturdy lock box, hidden away and bolted to wall studs, floorboards or such a large piece of furniture that it cannot be removed is essential. While you should be able to trust your housemates, you cannot know whom they will bring into the shared home as guests, and not only may you need physical defense from them, you also need security against theft. Do not keep a gun in shared housing unless you can secure it behind lock and key.

THE MOMMY YEARS

As women transition into motherhood, defense needs grow beyond self defense into providing safety for children, too. While armed women understandably hone defense skills to deal with not only attacks against themselves, but also work out defense strategies to protect their children, the safety concerns that attach to raising young children in an armed household arise. Lock boxes and gun safes remain of paramount importance for gun storage. Still, a gun locked in a safe is of little use if a threat comes into the back yard when you're out there roughhousing with your children.

Holsters with additional security measures make a lot of sense during the Mommy stage of life. That may call for the addition of a simple thumb-break strap snapping across the top of the holster or something more sophisticated like Bianchi's Auto Retention™ CarryLok™ or Galco's Matrix design that locks the gun in the holster until the hand drawing the gun presses against a paddle adjacent to the grips to release the lock. Alternatively, holsters that carry the gun beneath several layers of clothing may also do the trick of keeping curious little fingers away from the gun you are carrying for their defense and your own.

Galco's Matrix gun lock holster.

Many years ago Massad Ayoob wrote the child gun safety manual *Gun Safe Your Children*.[1] This is not our immediate topic, so let me simply point parents to that resource as well as the child-safe articles on www.corneredcat.com because there are complications unique to armed parents that are not specific to concealed carry. For the tots themselves, the National Rifle Association's Eddie Eagle program[2] is full of salient information presented in a child-friendly format that even the smallest family member can begin to parrot so that the principles of gun safety sink in as they grow old enough to understand what is at risk. The Eddie Eagle video is a golden oldie that has done an awful lot of good. You can get started with the animated version found on YouTube.

CAREER YEARS

An overlay to most of our adult years is work, career and firming up our financial standing. Naturally, the type of job you do influences the particular concealment challenges you must solve. Often, going to work calls for deep concealment balanced with accessibility, so that discovering you carry a gun does not discomfit coworkers and clients. Workplaces nearly always impose a formal or informal dress code, to which you will need to match the normal wardrobe pieces to several of the handgun concealment solutions we've already outlined.

Carrying a gun does not mean that you need to appear odd or different from your coworkers and peers. Adapt one part of your ensemble, say your blouses, to camouflage a small, flat handgun carried in a bellyband or Flashbang holster below the bust line. Use ruffled and gathered blouses, in this example.

If defaulting to a holster handbag to carry a gun to work, be sure you have a locker or locking desk drawer to keep the gun secure after you put your bag down and start your day's tasks.

RECREATION

Concealed carry solutions used during recreational pursuits apply all life long, and as you move into an active retirement you may find yourself using these options more and more. With moderate physical activity, the biggest holster problem is movement—flopping up and down. When activities entail a lot of movement, as may be faced by a runner, you may do best with a bellyband, waist pack or pocket carry of a small, light backup-type handgun. The smaller gun is a compromise that gives up much in user friendliness, so do not fail to practice and train to overcome these disadvantages as much as possible.

Naturally, there will be situations where your gun may be secured in a locker, while you swim laps, for example. Bear in mind that a handgun is only one facet of a larger personal safety lifestyle. While we carry a gun when legal and practical, women also need a repertoire of hand-to-hand defenses for the times when a gun cannot be kept immediately accessible.

Many youthful retirees travel extensively, and these armed citizens bless the flexibility granted by a concealed carry permit or license that is recognized by a number of states. At the time of writing, the Utah, Florida and Arizona per-

Springfield Armory's easy to use Model XDM-9

mits are commonly used by nonresidents not only while they are visiting those states, if they go there at all, but for the recognition granted those permits by other states.

THE GOLDEN YEARS

The golden years aren't always so golden! Age and infirmity can make the strongest of us look like easy prey to a predator. A discretely carried but accessible handgun becomes all the more important to active seniors. Fortunately, most senior women will have a little more latitude with fashion, so carry in a waist pack, kangaroo pouch holster or conventional belt holster is less intrusive than for the youthful fashionista.

More challenging is accessibility under disadvantageous circumstances, as may become needful if knocked down, pushed up against your car or otherwise attacked with overwhelming physical force. Also of greater importance to senior women is a handgun you can operate if hand strength and dexterity is diminished. Instead of a single-action semi-auto with the requirement to disengage a small safety, you may go to a Glock or Springfield Armory XD for easier shootability.

Many advise the double-action revolver on the premise that women struggle to cycle the slide of a semi-automatic handgun. This may have some merit, though we often see ladies in classes who find the revolver's 10- to 14-pound double action trigger pull requires more hand strength than they have. Sometimes a gunsmith can reduce the trigger pull somewhat, though there are limits to how much pull weight reduction is practical before the revolver becomes picky about what brands of ammunition it will discharge, owing to the hardness of the primers. Still, if you prefer the revolver to a semi-automatic, find a qualified gunsmith and ask what can be done to ease your struggle to pull the trigger.

Older armed citizens may make the compromise down to a smaller caliber, as well, if practice and training with a larger center fire caliber hurts hands and arms for days after live fire practice or completing a training course. Remember, compromises mean we are giving up something, so if downsizing to a smaller, more manageable caliber, your marksmanship and accuracy skills will need to take up the slack.

We have discussed a wide variety of guns and carry methods. In light of all the things women do and places women go, we should be grateful the market for concealed carry goods offers so many options.

(1) Gunsafe your Children, published by Police Bookshelf, June 1986, ISBN 978- 0936279052

(2) National Rifle Association, Eddie Eagle Gun Safety Program, 11250 Waples Mill Road Fairfax, VA 22030, 1-800-672-3888, http://eddieeagle.nra.org

NO COMPROMISE

We make hundreds of decisions every day. Be sure the decisions you make enhance your safety! This includes avoiding dangers, and it means having a way to defend against that which you cannot avoid. Playing a guessing game that tries to predict when trouble may strike is foolhardy! Habitually and regularly carrying a gun for personal defense whenever and wherever legal is a sensible decision. We close out this book with encouragement to persevere even when carrying a gun for personal defense is inconvenient, uncomfortable or when doing so opens you up to criticism. Falling prey to a predator is considerably worse than any of those discomforts.

It is ironic that much of the advice about carrying a handgun for personal protection includes compromises:

– Compromises between the size of the gun and the clothing required to conceal it;

– Compromises in choices of activities to allow legal concealed carry for better personal safety;

– Compromises in physical comfort for the mental comfort of having a gun quickly at hand to fend off danger.

There is one compromise, though, that we must avoid. That is the compromise that is sometimes urged upon us as women to let others take responsibility for our safety. This "offer" is a lie because it simply is not reasonable to believe that another person can be continually present to provide your protection.

If you understand and accept that your safety is your own responsibility, and have chosen to carry a concealed handgun as part of your personal safety provisions, make the commitment to yourself to carry your gun consistently. The idea that we can predict when danger may strike is ridiculous and demonstrates how very foolish it is to carry your gun only when you find it convenient. Personal safety is a serious, no-compromise responsibility.

Carrying a gun is most successful when practiced consistently. Not only does this mean carrying regularly, it means working to carry in the same holster and body location as much as is possible. If you do appendix carry, use your holster there, position a belly band holster in a similar location, and if you ever use a purse, backpack or brief case holster, carry it forward of the hip on the same side as your conventional holster. As much as possible, avoid making big holster location changes, as might happen between carrying in an ankle holster one day, then a waist pack on the weekend, and a shoulder holster another day.

It may take a few years to convert your pre-gun wardrobe to one that works for maximum concealment, and you will in all likelihood go through several holsters before settling down to an "every day carry" option that you employ 90 percent of the time, with the other ten percent covered by alternative devices like the waist packs, belly bands and other options we've outlined. While it's unlikely that you'll be carrying the same gun and holster ten years from now, by purchasing high-quality gear, you can probably keep the changes and upgrades in the single digits instead of going through dozens of options before settling down on two or three.

Learning through observation and listening to others is useful, yet know that in the end you have to make your own decisions about what you are safe and comfortable carrying for personal protection. Be very suspicious of strongly opinionated people who are all too willing to tell you what the "perfect" gun and holster combination is for you. How can they know? Using the principles that we've discussed throughout this book, establish your own style, your own high standards, and settle into a routine of consistently carrying your personal defense handgun. Consistency pays big dividends in familiarity, focusing your practice and training time, and readiness if ever you must use your defense gear and skills to avoid falling victim to violent crime.

When you start to feel overwhelmed by the challenges of equipment selection, skills acquisition and maintenance, and all the other factors that go into personal safety, break the problems down into small challenges and master one at a time. Remember, women, we have been solving problems all our lives with feminine creativity, working through the steps to problem resolution, thinking outside the box, and applying sheer perseverance. Carrying a gun for personal protection requires the same skills. This is your challenge! Do you have the commitment?

ABOUT
THE AUTHOR

Gila Hayes came to the study of firearms for self defense upon recognition that dangers posed by violent crime exceeded the defense skills she'd learned in the martial arts dojo. Intense study of armed self defense ensued, leading to training with Massad Ayoob, John Farnam, Louis Awerbuck, Clint Smith, Chuck Taylor, Ken Hackathorn, Jim Cirillo, and others. She went on to complete instructor programs including Staff Instructor for the Lethal Force Institute, certification through the National Law Enforcement Training Center, the Heckler and Koch International Training Division, Washington State Criminal Justice Training Commission's Police Firearms Instructor certification, American Women's Self Defense Association, and the National Rifle Association. Twice, she has taught at the annual training conference of the American Society of Law Enforcement Trainers and has presented at the International Association of Law Enforcement Firearms Instructors' regional training conference.

Since 1993, she has been a staff instructor for the Firearms Academy of Seattle, teaching gun safety and armed self defense in both the handgun and shotgun programs at the academy. She served as a reserve police officer between 1997 and 2007, primarily tasked with providing firearms training.

Hayes is one of three founding leaders of the Armed Citizens' Legal Defense Network, Inc., a membership organization formed for the legal protection of Network members after using deadly force in self defense. Education to increase understanding of issues relating to use of deadly force in self defense as well as the follow-on legal issues is a big part of the Network's more immediate services to members. To this end, Hayes produces a monthly journal published online at www.armedcitizensnetwork. org as well as overseeing the day-to-day operation of the Network.

In addition to *Personal Defense for Women* (Gun Digest Books, 2009) and *Effective Defense* (self-published, 2nd edition 2000), Hayes was field editor for *Women & Guns* magazine writing one to two articles per month for over ten years, and wrote for *Gun Digest* (2010, 2012), *Police Magazine, Handguns, NRA American Guardian* and *Woman's Outlook, American Handgunner, Gun Week, GUNS Magazine, Combat Handguns Annual, Glock Annual, Smith & Wesson Annual* and others.